EAS ANGL

C000121323

Regional Road Atlas

CONTENTS

Key to Map Pages............2-3
Road Maps.....................4-42

Index to Towns and Villages......43-54
Index to Places of Interest......... 55-64

REFERENCE

MOTORWAY	M1
Under Construction	
Proposed	
MOTORWAY JUNCTIONS WITH NUMBERS	
Unlimited interchange 6 Limited interchange 7	
MOTORWAY SERVICE AREA	SOUTH MIMMS Ⓢ
with access from one carriageway only	Ⓢ
MAJOR ROAD SERVICE AREAS	BABRAHAM GRASBY
with 24 hour Facilities	Ⓢ Ⓢ
PRIMARY ROUTE	A14
PRIMARY ROUTE DESTINATION	DISS
DUAL CARRIAGEWAY (A & B Roads)	
CLASS A ROAD	A143
CLASS B ROAD	B1113
MAJOR ROAD UNDER CONSTRUCTION	
MAJOR ROAD PROPOSED	
GRADIENT 1:5(20%) & STEEPER (Ascent in direction of arrow)	≪
TOLL	TOLL
MILEAGE BETWEEN MARKERS	8
RAILWAY AND STATION	
LEVEL CROSSING AND TUNNEL	
RIVER OR CANAL	
COUNTY OR UNITARY AUTHORITY BOUNDARY	
NATIONAL BOUNDARY	
BUILT UP AREA	
VILLAGE OR HAMLET	
WOODED AREA	
SPOT HEIGHT IN FEET	• 813
HEIGHT ABOVE SEA LEVEL 400'-1,000' 122m-305m 1,000'-1,400' 305m-427m 1,400'-2,000' 427m-610m 2,000'+ 610m +	
NATIONAL GRID REFERENCE (Kilometres)	100

TOURIST INFORMATION

AIRPORT	✈
AIRFIELD	✈
HELIPORT	⊀
BATTLE SITE AND DATE	⚔ 1066
CASTLE (Open to Public)	🏰
CASTLE WITH GARDEN (Open to Public)	🏰
CATHEDRAL, ABBEY, CHURCH, FRIARY, PRIORY	✝
COUNTRY PARK	🌲
FERRY (Vehicular)	⛴
(Foot only)	🚶
GARDEN (Open to Public)	❀
GOLF COURSE 9 HOLE 18 HOLE	⛳
HISTORIC BUILDING (Open to Public)	🏛
HISTORIC BUILDING WITH GARDEN (Open to Public)	🏛
HORSE RACECOURSE	🏇
INFORMATION CENTRE	🅸
LIGHTHOUSE	🗼
MOTOR RACING CIRCUIT	
MUSEUM, ART GALLERY	🖼
NATIONAL PARK OR FOREST PARK	
NATIONAL TRUST PROPERTY (Open)	NT
(Restricted Opening)	NT
(National Trust of Scotland)	NTS NTS
NATURE RESERVE OR BIRD SANCTUARY	
NATURE TRAIL OR FOREST WALK	♣
PLACE OF INTEREST Monument	•
PICNIC SITE	⛱
RAILWAY, STEAM OR NARROW GAUGE	
THEME PARK	
VIEWPOINT	☀ ☀
WILDLIFE PARK	Y
WINDMILL	X
ZOO OR SAFARI PARK	🐘

SCALE

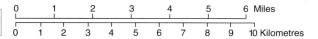

1:158,400
2.5 Miles to 1 Inch

Geographers' A-Z Map Company Ltd

Head Office : (General Enquiries & Trade Sales)
Fairfield Road, Borough Green, Sevenoaks,
Kent TN15 8PP Telephone: 01732- 781000
Showroom : (Retail Sales)
44 Gray's Inn Road, London, WC1X 8HX
Telephone: 020- 7440 9500

Edition 5 2001 Copyright Ⓒ Geographers' A-Z Map Company Ltd.

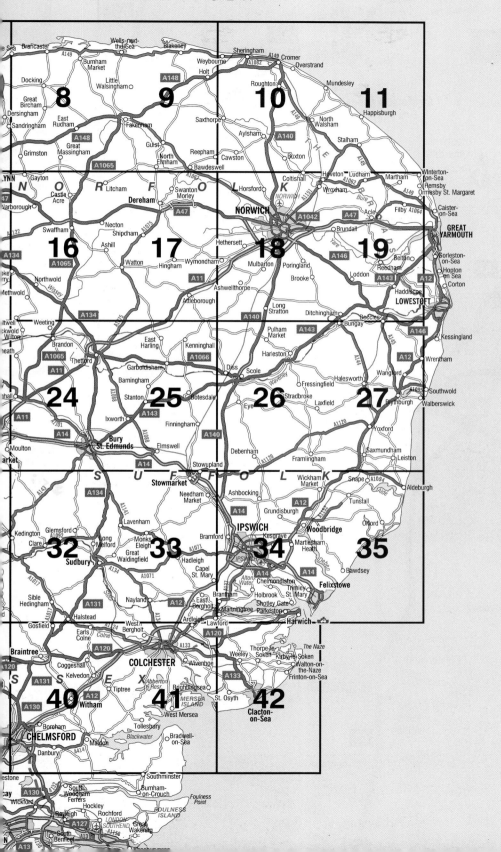

NORTH SEA

3

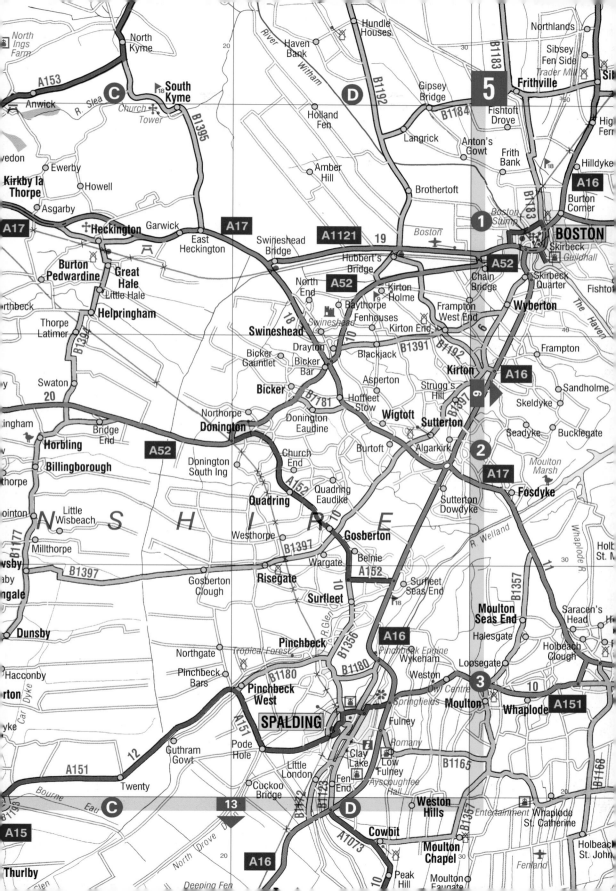

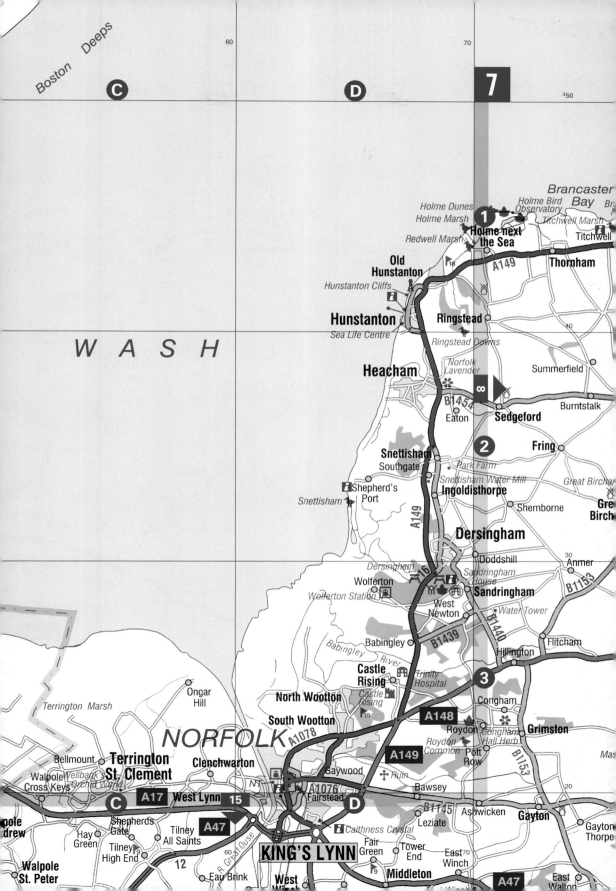

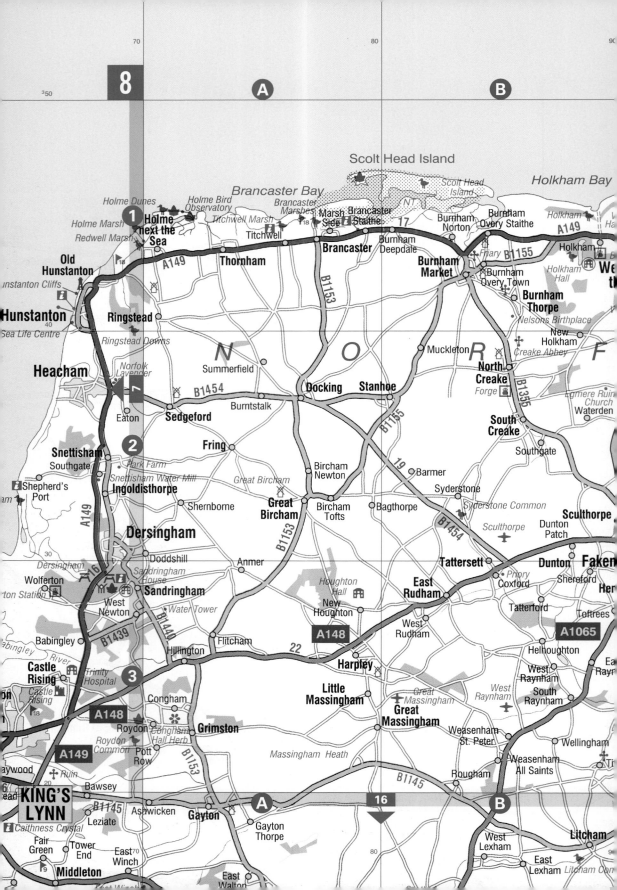

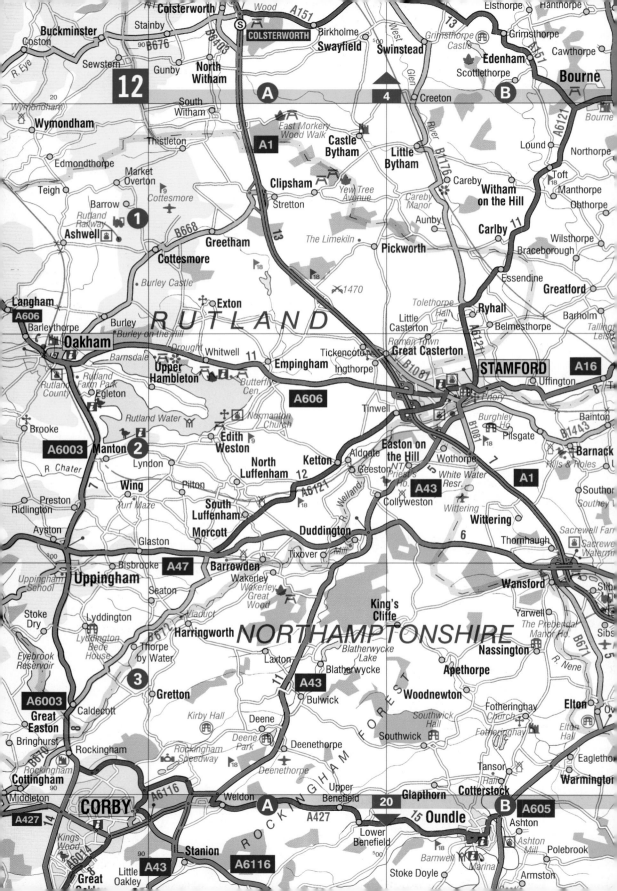

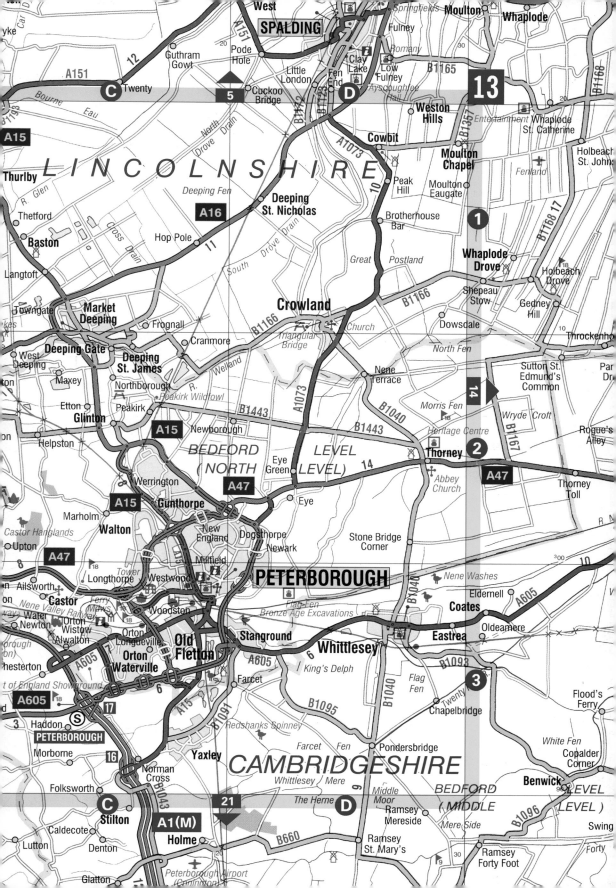

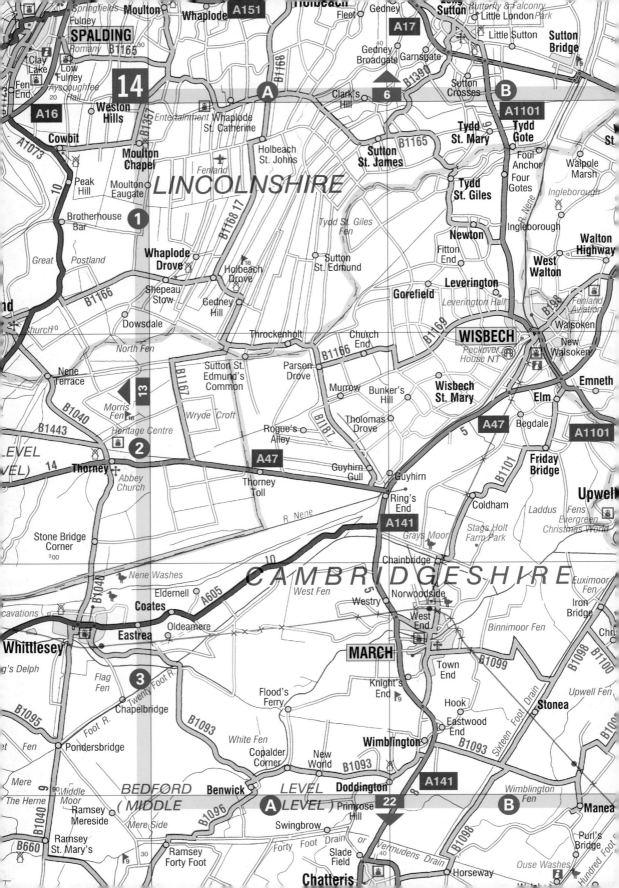

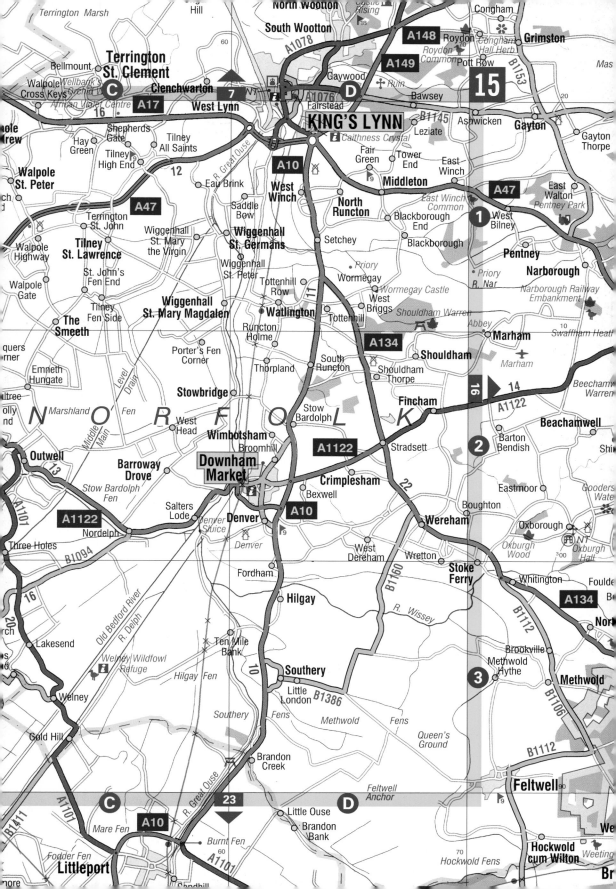

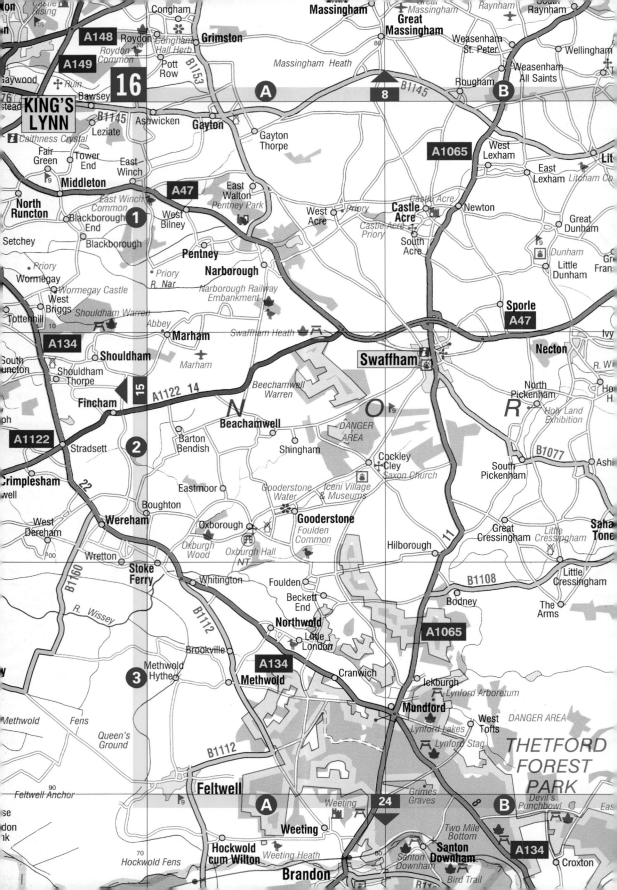

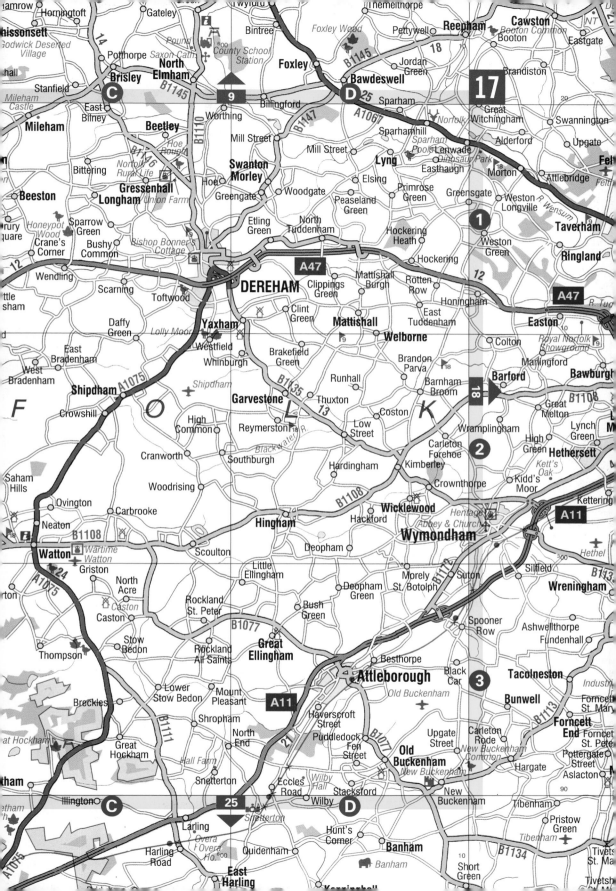

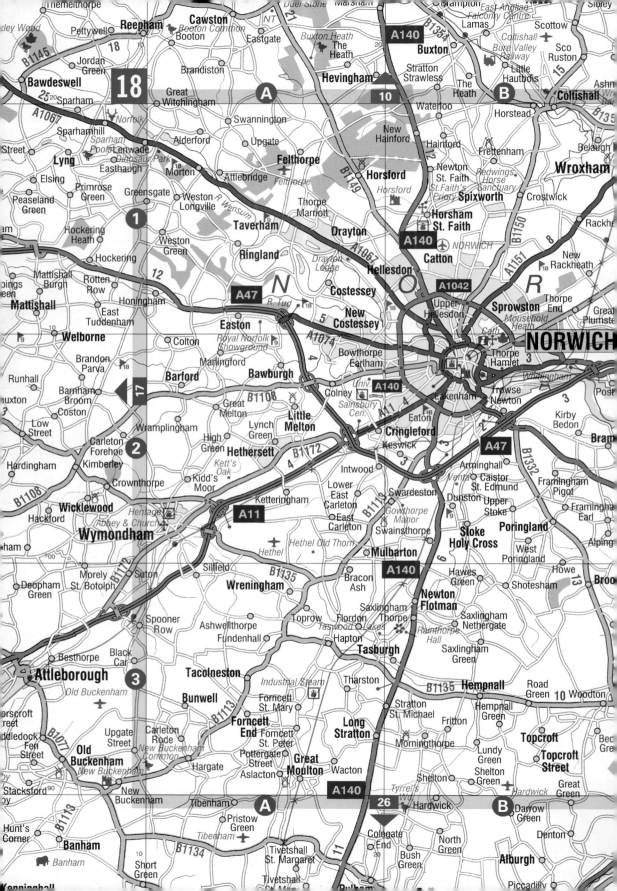

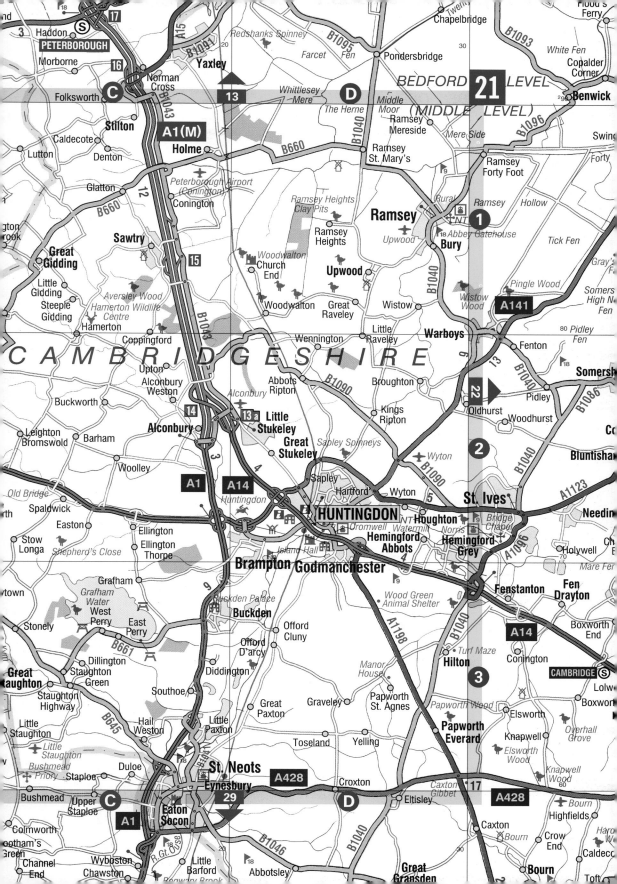

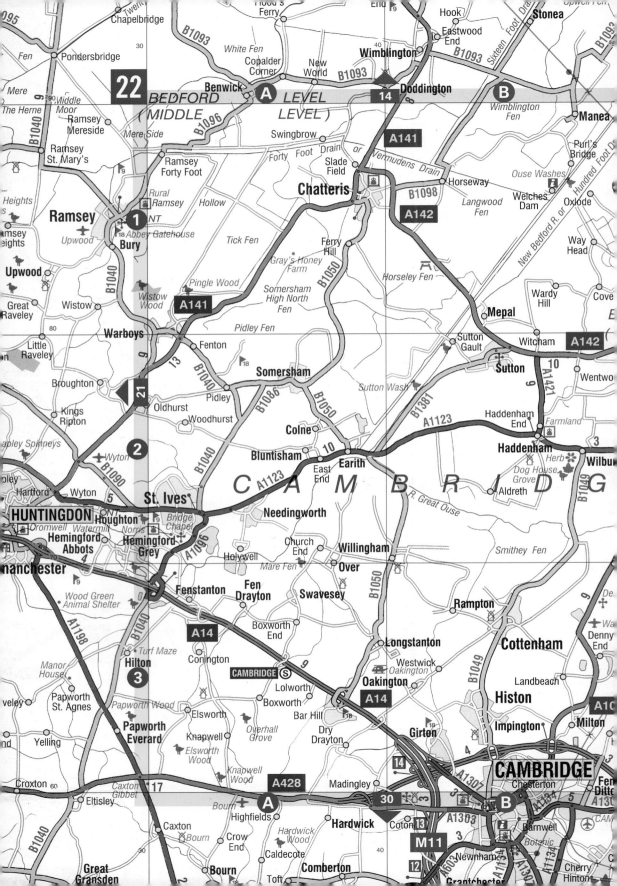

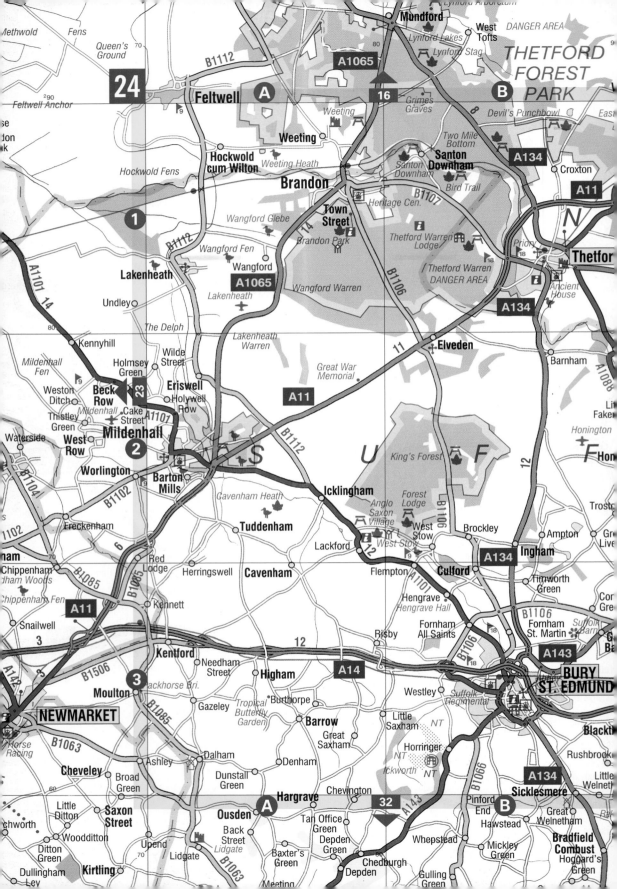

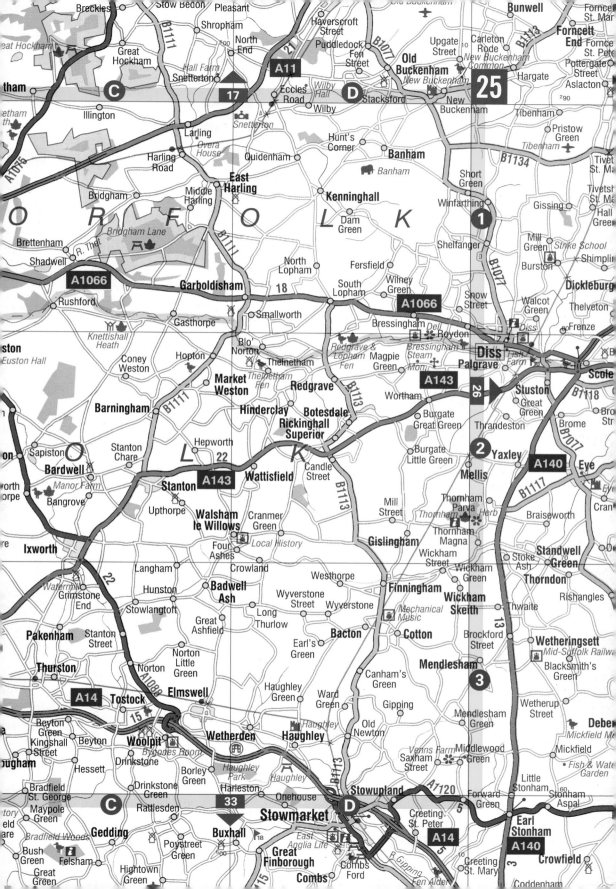

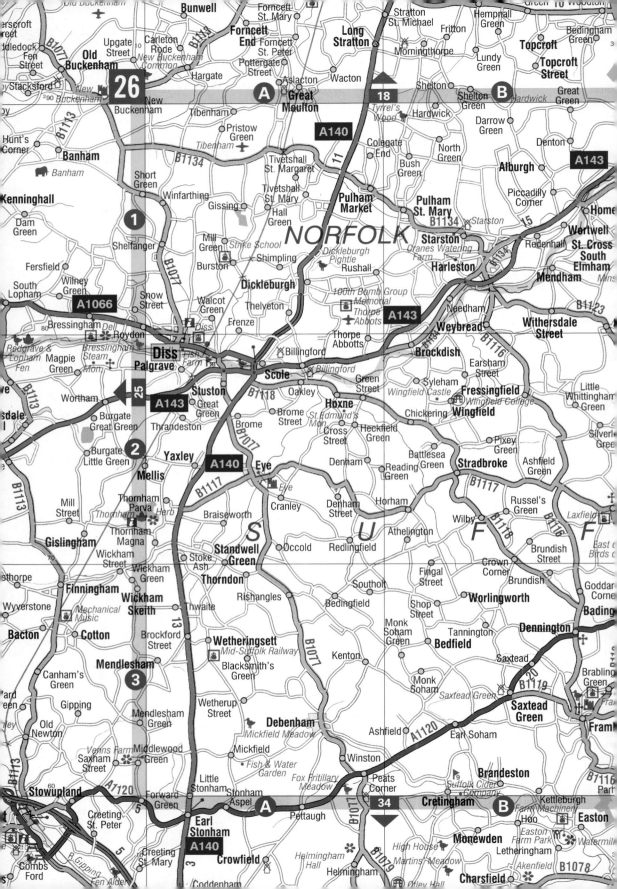

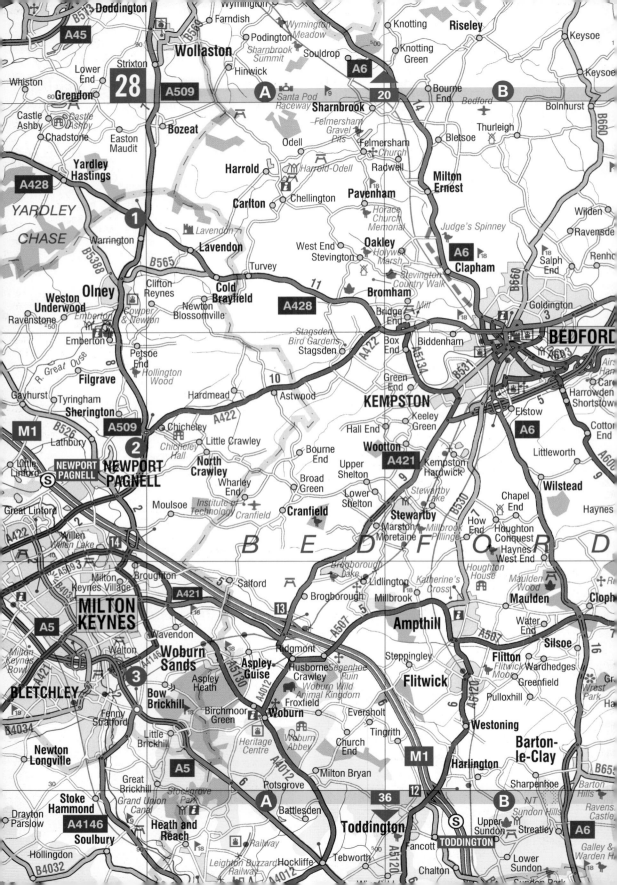

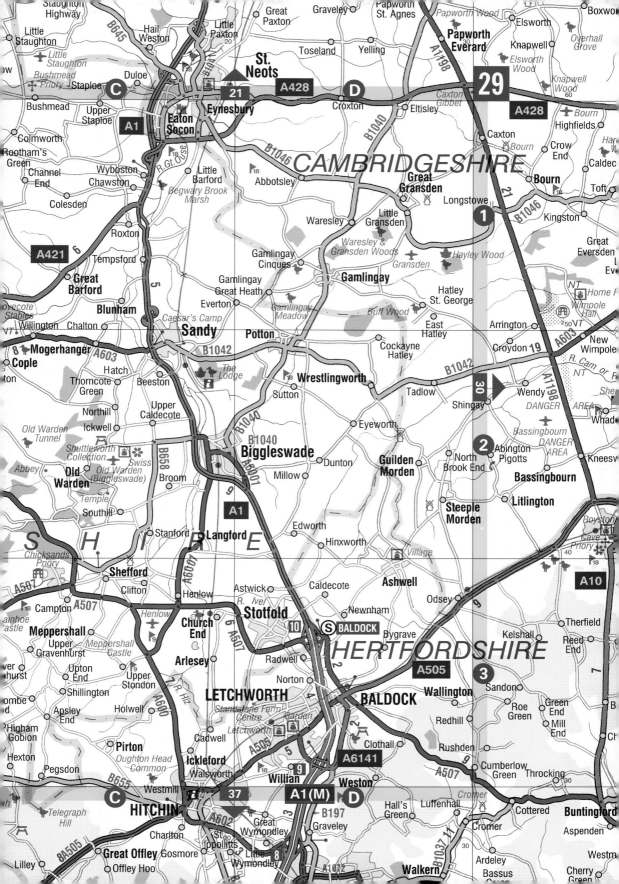

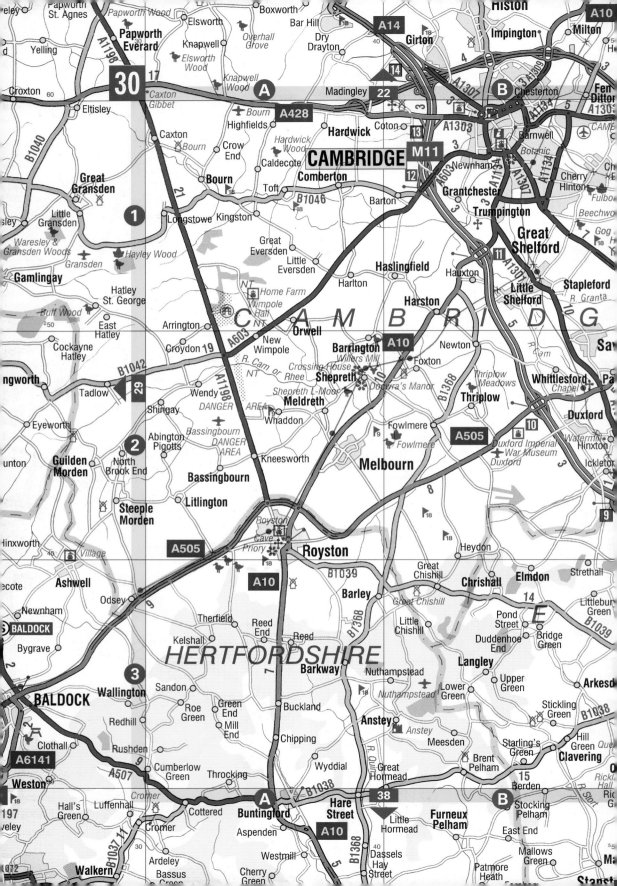

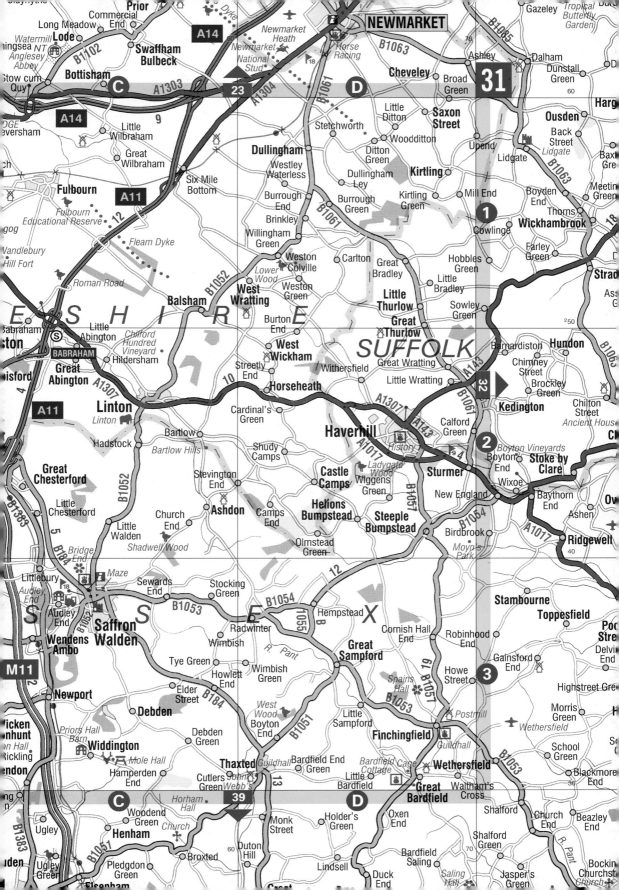

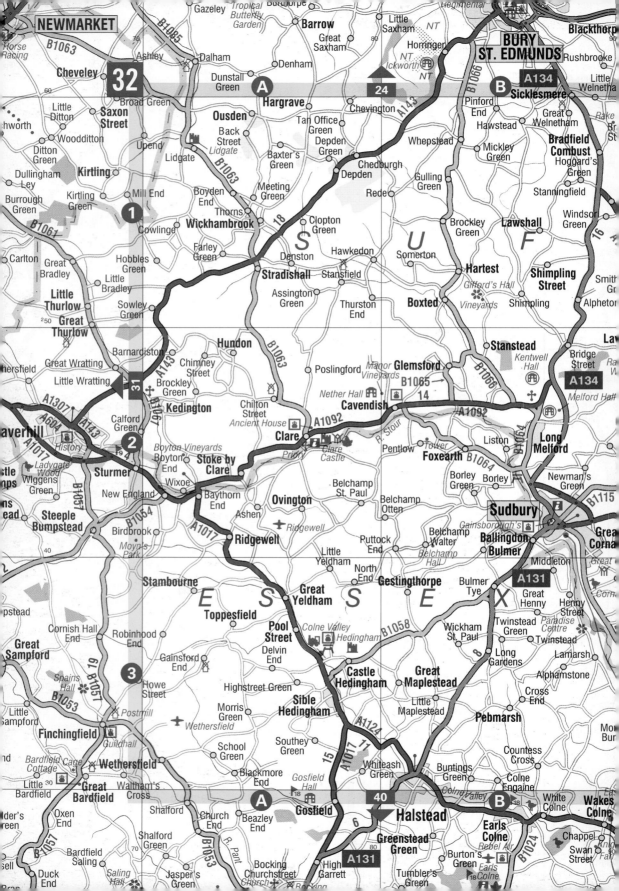

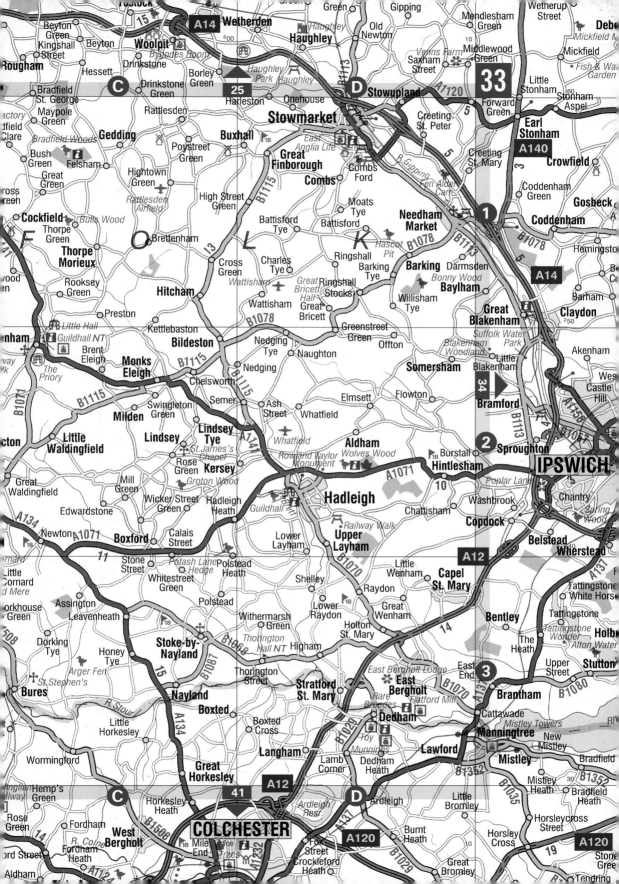

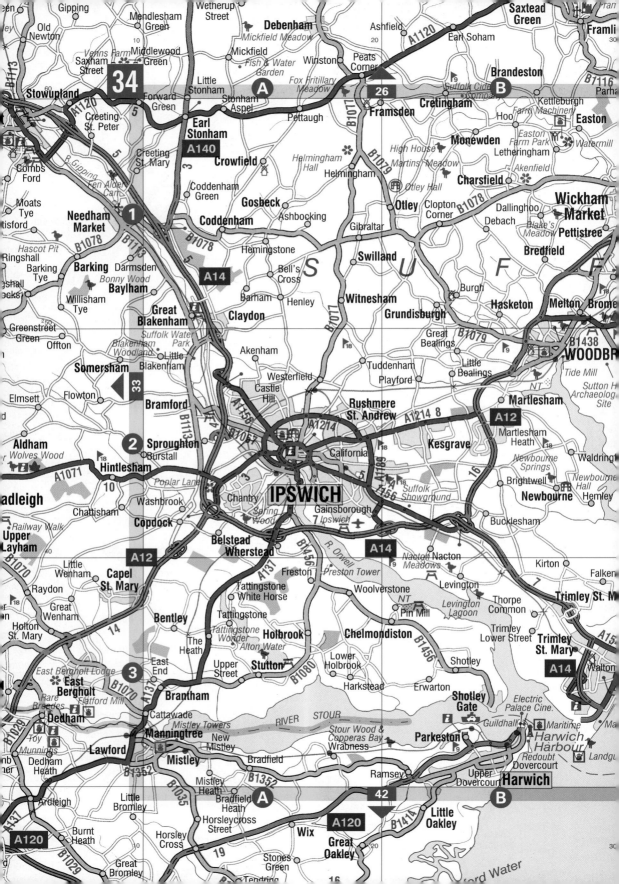

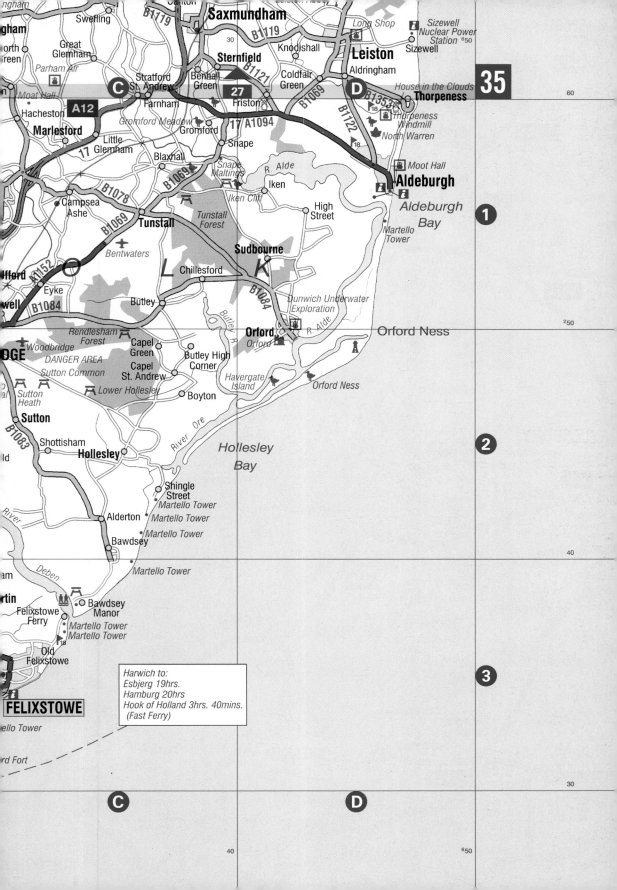

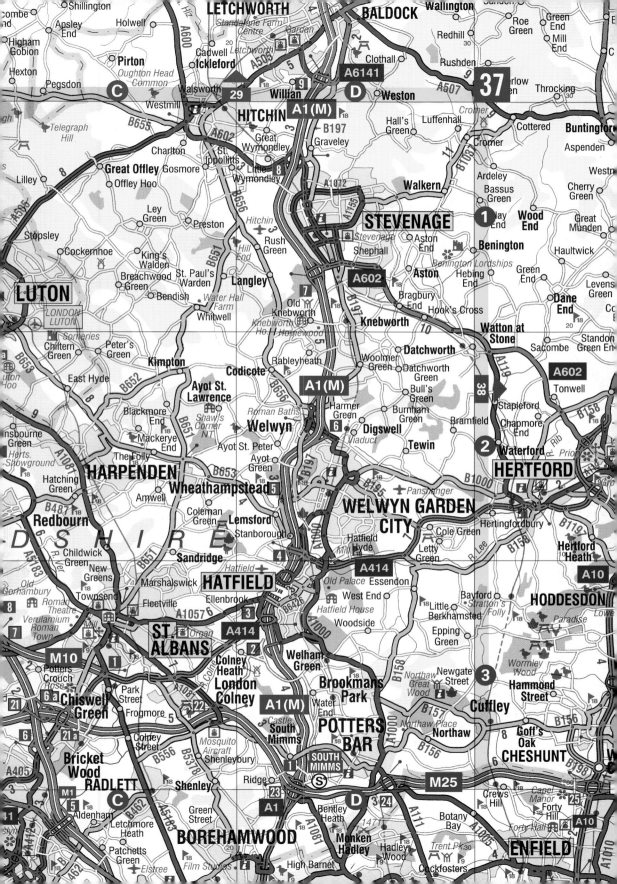

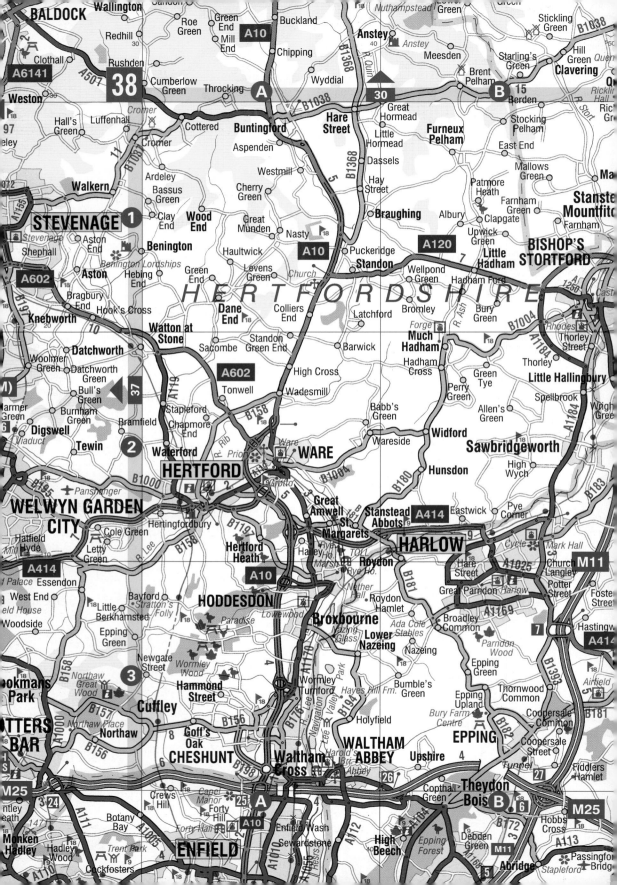

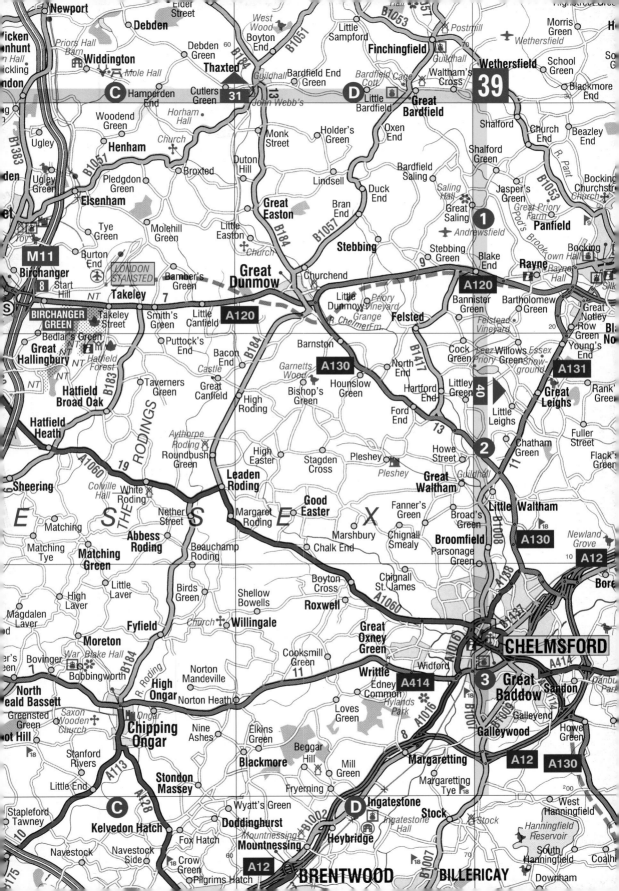

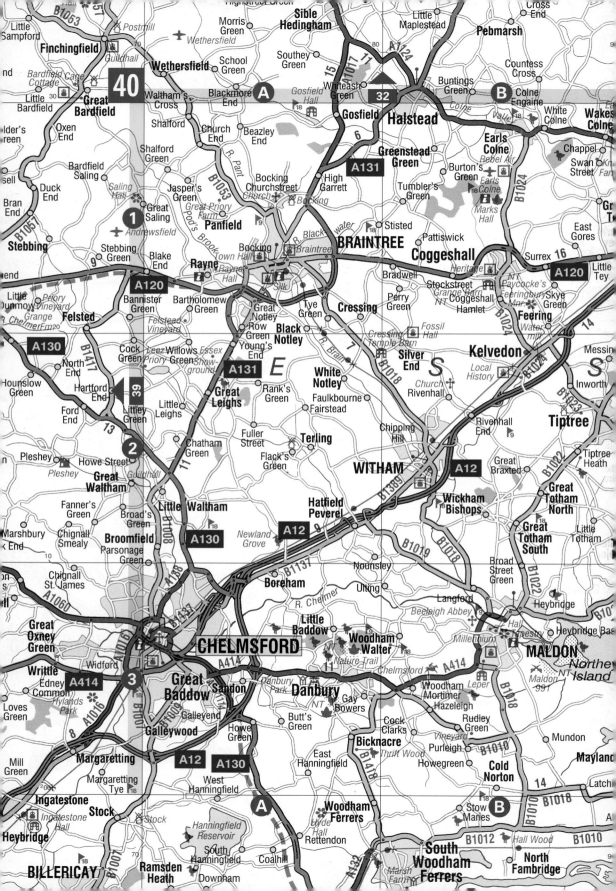

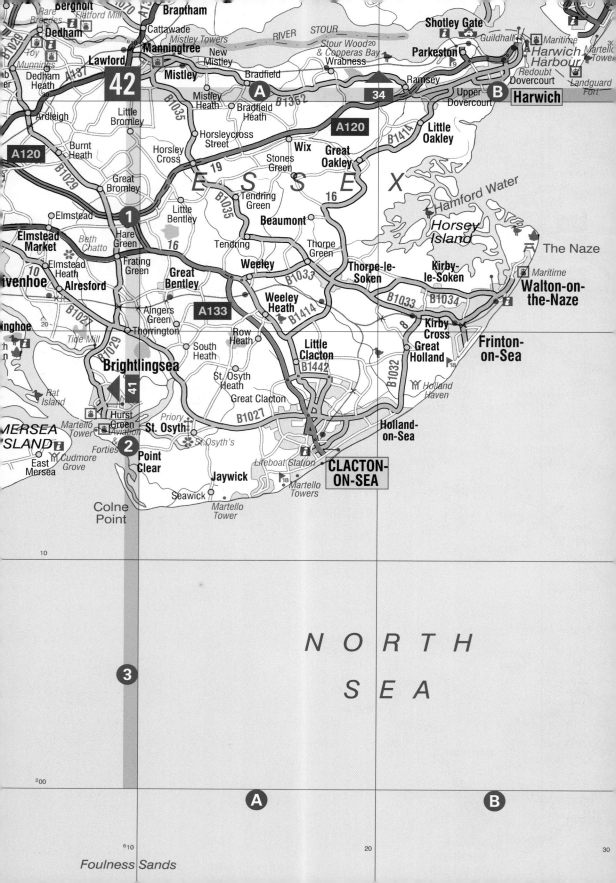

INDEX TO CITIES, TOWNS, VILLAGES, HAMLETS & LOCATIONS

(1) A strict alphabetical order is used e.g. Abbotsley follows Abbots Langley but precedes Abbots Ripton.

(2) The map reference given refers to the actual map square in which the town spot or built-up area is located and not to the place name.

(3) Where two places of the same name occur in the same County or Unitary Authority, the nearest large town is also given; e.g. Billingford. *Norf* —2A **26** (nr. Diss) indicates that Billingford is located in square 2A on page **26** and is situated near Diss in the County of Norfolk.

COUNTIES AND UNITARY AUTHORITIES with the abbreviations used in this index.

Bedfordshire : *Beds*
Buckinghamshire : *Buck*
Cambridgeshire : *Cambs*
Cornwall : *Corn*

Essex : *Essx*
Greater London : *G Lon*
Hertfordshire : *Herts*
Leicestershire : *Leics*

Lincolnshire : *Linc*
Luton : *Lutn*
Milton Keynes : *Mil*
Norfolk : *Norf*

Northamptonshire : *Nptn*
Nottinghamshire : *Notts*
Oxfordshire : *Oxon*
Peterborough : *Pet*

Rutland : *Rut*
Suffolk : *Suff*

Abberton. *Essx* —2D **41**
Abbess Roding. *Essx* —2C **39**
Abbots Langley. *Herts* —3B **36**
Abbotsley. *Cambs* —1D **29**
Abbots Ripton. *Cambs* —2D **21**
Abington Pigotts. *Cambs* —2A **30**
Abridge. *Essx* —3B **38**
Achurch. *Nptn* —1B **20**
Acle. *Norf* —1D **19**
Acton. *Suff* —2B **32**
Ailsworth. *Pet* —3C **13**
Aingers Green. *Essx* —1A **42**
Aisby. *Linc* —2B **4**
Akenham. *Suff* —2A **34**
Alburgh. *Norf* —1B **26**
Albury. *Herts* —1B **38**
Alby Hill. *Norf* —2A **10**
Alconbury. *Cambs* —2C **21**
Alconbury Weston. *Cambs* —2C **21**
Aldborough. *Norf* —2A **10**
Aldbury. *Herts* —2A **36**
Aldeburgh. *Suff* —1D **35**
Aldeby. *Norf* —3D **19**
Aldenham. *Herts* —3C **37**
Alderford. *Norf* —1A **18**
Alderton. *Suff* —2C **35**
Aldgate. *Rut* —2A **12**
Aldham. *Essx* —1C **41**
Aldham. *Suff* —2D **33**
Aldreth. *Cambs* —2B **22**
Aldringham. *Suff* —3D **27**
Aldwincle. *Nptn* —2C **21**
Aley Green. *Beds* —2B **36**
Algarkirk. *Linc* —2D **5**
Allen's Green. *Herts* —2B **38**
Allington. *Linc* —1A **4**
All Saints South Elmham. *Suff* —1C **27**
Alphamstone. *Essx* —3B **32**
Alpheton. *Suff* —1B **32**
Alpington. *Norf* —2B **18**
Alresford. *Essx* —1D **41**
Althorne. *Essx* —3C **41**
Alwalton. *Pet* —3C **13**
Amber Hill. *Linc* —1D **5**
Amersham. *Buck* —3A **36**
Ampthill. *Beds* —3B **28**
Ampton. *Suff* —2B **24**
Amwell. *Herts* —2C **37**
Ancaster. *Linc* —1A **4**
Anmer. *Norf* —3A **8**
Anstey. *Herts* —3B **30**
Antingham. *Norf* —2B **10**
Anton's Gowt. *Linc* —1D **5**
Anwick. *Linc* —1C **5**
Apethorpe. *Nptn* —3B **12**
Apsley End. *Beds* —3C **29**

Ardeley. *Herts* —1A **38**
Ardleigh. *Essx* —1D **41**
Arkesden. *Essx* —3B **30**
Arlesey. *Beds* —3C **29**
Arminghall. *Norf* —2B **18**
Arms, The. *Norf* —3B **16**
Armston. *Nptn* —1B **20**
Arrington. *Cambs* —1A **30**
Asgarby. *Linc* —1C **5**
Ashbocking. *Suff* —1A **34**
Ashby St Mary. *Norf* —2C **19**
Ashdon. *Essx* —2C **31**
Asheldham. *Essx* —3C **41**
Ashen. *Essx* —2A **32**
Ashfield. *Suff* —3B **26**
Ashfield Green. *Suff* —2B **26**
Ashill. *Norf* —2B **16**
Ashley. *Cambs* —3D **23**
Ashley Green. *Buck* —3A **36**
Ashmanhaugh. *Norf* —3C **11**
Ash Street. *Suff* —2D **33**
Ashton. *Nptn* —1B **20**
Ashton. *Pet* —2C **13**
Ashwell. *Herts* —3B **29**
Ashwell. *Rut* —1A **12**
Ashwellthorpe. *Norf* —3A **18**
Ashwicken. *Norf* —1A **16**
Aslackby. *Linc* —2B **4**
Aslacton. *Norf* —3A **18**
Aspenden. *Herts* —1A **38**
Asperton. *Linc* —2D **5**
Aspley Guise. *Beds* —3A **28**
Aspley Heath. *Beds* —3A **28**
Assington. *Suff* —3C **33**
Assington Green. *Suff* —1A **32**
Aston. *Herts* —1D **37**
Aston Abbotts. *Buck* —1A **36**
Aston Clinton. *Buck* —2A **36**
Aston End. *Herts* —1D **37**
Astwick. *Beds* —3D **29**
Astwood. *Mil* —2A **28**
Aswarby. *Linc* —2B **4**
Athelington. *Suff* —2B **26**
Attleborough. *Norf* —3D **17**
Attlebridge. *Norf* —1A **18**
Audley End. *Essx* —3C **31**
Aunby. *Linc* —1B **12**
Aunsby. *Linc* —2B **4**
Aylmerton. *Norf* —2A **10**
Aylsham. *Norf* —3A **10**
Ayot Green. *Herts* —2D **37**
Ayot St Lawrence. *Herts* —2C **37**
Ayot St Peter. *Herts* —2D **37**
Ayston. *Rut* —2A **12**

Babb's Green. *Herts* —2A **38**
Babingley. *Norf* —3D **7**

Babraham. *Cambs* —1C **31**
Back Street. *Suff* —1A **32**
Bacon End. *Essx* —2D **39**
Baconsthorpe. *Norf* —2A **10**
Bacton. *Norf* —2C **11**
Bacton. *Suff* —3D **25**
Bacton Green. *Norf* —2C **11**
Badingham. *Suff* —3C **27**
Badwell Ash. *Suff* —3C **25**
Bagthorpe. *Norf* —2A **8**
Bainton. *Pet* —2B **12**
Baldock. *Herts* —3D **29**
Bale. *Norf* —2D **9**
Ballingdon. *Suff* —2B **32**
Ballingdon Bulmer. *Essx* —2B **32**
Ballinger Common. *Buck* —3A **36**
Balsham. *Cambs* —1C **31**
Bamber's Green. *Essx* —1C **39**
Bangrove. *Suff* —2C **25**
Banham. *Norf* —1D **25**
Banningham. *Norf* —3B **10**
Bannister Green. *Essx* —1D **39**
Banyard's Green. *Suff* —2C **27**
Bardfield End Green. *Essx* —3D **31**
Bardfield Saling. *Essx* —1D **39**
Bardwell. *Suff* —2C **25**
Barford. *Norf* —2A **18**
Barham. *Cambs* —2C **21**
Barham. *Suff* —1A **34**
Bar Hill. *Cambs* —3A **22**
Barholm. *Linc* —1B **12**
Barking. *Suff* —1D **33**
Barking Tye. *Suff* —1D **33**
Barkston. *Linc* —1A **4**
Barkway. *Herts* —3A **30**
Barley. *Herts* —3A **30**
Barleythorpe. *Rut* —2A **12**
Barmer. *Norf* —2B **8**
Barnack. *Pet* —2B **12**
Barnardiston. *Suff* —2A **32**
Barnby. *Suff* —1D **27**
Barnby in the Willows. *Notts* —1A **4**
Barnet. *G Lon* —3D **37**
Barney. *Norf* —2C **9**
Barnham. *Suff* —2B **24**
Barnham Broom. *Norf* —2D **17**
Barningham. *Suff* —2C **25**
Barnston. *Essx* —2D **39**
Barnwell. *Cambs* —1B **30**
Barnwell All Saints. *Nptn* —1B **20**

Barnwell St Andrew. *Nptn* —1B **20**
Barrington. *Cambs* —2A **30**
Barrow. *Rut* —1A **12**
Barrow. *Suff* —3A **24**
Barroway Drove. *Norf* —2C **15**
Barrowby. *Linc* —2A **4**
Barrowden. *Rut* —2A **12**
Barsham. *Suff* —1C **27**
Bartholomew Green. *Essx* —1A **40**
Bartlow. *Cambs* —2C **31**
Barton. *Cambs* —1B **30**
Barton Bendish. *Norf* —2A **16**
Barton-le-Clay. *Beds* —3B **28**
Barton Mills. *Suff* —2A **24**
Barton Seagrave. *Nptn* —2A **20**
Barton Turf. *Norf* —3C **11**
Barway. *Cambs* —2C **23**
Barwick. *Herts* —2A **38**
Bassingbourn. *Cambs* —2A **30**
Bassingthorpe. *Linc* —3A **4**
Bassus Green. *Herts* —1A **38**
Baston. *Linc* —1C **13**
Bastwick. *Norf* —1D **19**
Battisford. *Suff* —1D **33**
Battisford Tye. *Suff* —1D **33**
Battlesden. *Beds* —1A **36**
Battlesea Green. *Suff* —2B **26**
Bawburgh. *Norf* —2A **18**
Bawdeswell. *Norf* —3D **9**
Bawdsey. *Suff* —2C **35**
Bawdsey Manor. *Suff* —3C **35**
Bawsey. *Norf* —1D **15**
Baxter's Green. *Suff* —1A **32**
Bayford. *Herts* —3A **38**
Baylham. *Suff* —1A **34**
Baythorn End. *Essx* —2A **32**
Baythorpe. *Linc* —1D **5**
Beachamwell. *Norf* —2A **16**
Beacon End. *Essx* —1C **41**
Beamond End. *Buck* —3A **36**
Beauchamp Roding. *Essx* —2C **39**
Beaumont. *Essx* —1A **42**
Beazley End. *Essx* —1A **40**
Beccles. *Suff* —1D **27**
Beckett End. *Norf* —3A **16**
Beckingham. *Linc* —1A **4**
Beck Row. *Suff* —2D **23**
Bedfield. *Suff* —3B **26**
Bedford. *Beds* —2B **28**
Bedingfield. *Suff* —3A **26**
Bedingham Green. *Norf* —3B **18**

Bedlar's Green. *Essx* —1C **39**
Bedmond. *Herts* —3B **36**
Beeston. *Beds* —2C **29**
Beeston. *Norf* —1C **17**
Beeston Regis. *Norf* —1A **10**
Beetley. *Norf* —1C **17**
Begdale. *Cambs* —2B **14**
Beggar Hill. *Essx* —3D **39**
Beighton. *Norf* —2C **19**
Belaugh. *Norf* —1B **18**
Belchamp Otten. *Essx* —2B **32**
Belchamp St Paul. *Essx* —2A **32**
Belchamp Walter. *Essx* —2B **32**
Bellingdon. *Buck* —3A **36**
Bellmount. *Norf* —3C **7**
Bell's Cross. *Suff* —1A **34**
Belmesthorpe. *Rut* —1B **12**
Belnie. *Linc* —2D **5**
Belsize. *Herts* —3B **36**
Belstead. *Suff* —2A **34**
Belton. *Linc* —2A **4**
Belton. *Norf* —2D **19**
Benacre. *Suff* —1D **27**
Bendish. *Herts* —1C **37**
Bengate. *Norf* —3C **11**
Benhall Green. *Suff* —3C **27**
Benington. *Herts* —1A **38**
Benington. *Linc* —1A **6**
Benington Sea End. *Linc* —1B **6**
Bentley. *Suff* —3A **34**
Bentley Heath. *Herts* —3D **37**
Benwick. *Cambs* —3A **14**
Berden. *Essx* —1B **38**
Bergh Apton. *Norf* —2C **19**
Berkhamstead. *Herts* —3D **37**
Berkhamsted. *Herts* —3A **36**
Bessingham. *Norf* —2A **10**
Besthorpe. *Norf* —3D **17**
Bexfield. *Norf* —3D **9**
Bexwell. *Norf* —2D **15**
Beyton. *Suff* —3C **25**
Beyton Green. *Suff* —3C **25**
Bicker. *Linc* —2D **5**
Bicker Bar. *Linc* —2D **5**
Bicker Gauntlet. *Linc* —2D **5**
Bicknacre. *Essx* —3A **40**
Biddenham. *Beds* —2B **28**
Bierton. *Buck* —2A **36**
Biggleswade. *Beds* —2C **29**
Bildeston. *Suff* —2C **33**
Billericay. *Essx* —3D **39**
Billingborough. *Linc* —2C **5**
Billingford. *Norf* —2A **26** (nr. Diss)
Billingford. *Norf* —3D **9** (nr. East Dereham)

Billington. *Beds* —1A **36**
Billockby. *Norf* —1D **19**
Binham. *Norf* —2C **9**
Bintree. *Norf* —3D **9**
Birch. *Essx* —2C **41**
Bircham Newton. *Norf*
—2A **8**
Bircham Tofts. *Norf* —2A **8**
Birchanger. *Essx* —1C **39**
Birch Green. *Essx* —2C **41**
Birchmoor Green. *Beds*
—3A **28**
Birdbrook. *Essx* —2A **32**
Birds Green. *Essx* —3C **39**
Birkholme. *Linc* —3A **4**
Birthorpe. *Linc* —2C **5**
Bisbrooke. *Rut* —3A **12**
Bishop's Green. *Essx*
—2D **39**
Bishop's Stortford. *Herts*
—1B **38**
Bitchfield. *Linc* —3A **4**
Bittering. *Norf* —1C **17**
Black Bank. *Cambs* —1C **23**
Black Barn. *Linc* —3B **6**
Blackborough. *Norf* —1D **15**
Blackborough End. *Norf*
—1D **15**
Black Car. *Norf* —3D **17**
Blackheath. *Essx* —1D **41**
Blackheath. *Suff* —2D **27**
Blackjack. *Linc* —2D **5**
Blackmore. *Essx* —3D **39**
Blackmore End. *Essx*
—3A **32**
Blackmore End. *Herts*
—2C **37**
Black Notley. *Essx* —1A **40**
Blacksmith's Green. *Suff*
—3A **26**
Black Street. *Suff* —1D **27**
Blackthorpe. *Suff* —3C **25**
Blake End. *Essx* —1A **40**
Blakeney. *Norf* —1D **9**
Blatherwycke. *Nptn* —3A **12**
Blaxhall. *Suff* —1C **35**
Bletchley. *Mil* —3A **28**
Bletsoe. *Beds* —1B **28**
Blickling. *Norf* —3A **10**
Blofield. *Norf* —2C **19**
Blofield Heath. *Norf* —1C **19**
Blo' Norton. *Norf* —2D **25**
Bloxholm. *Linc* —1B **4**
Blue Row. *Essx* —2D **41**
Blundeston. *Suff* —3D **19**
Blunham. *Beds* —1C **29**
Bluntisham. *Cambs* —2A **22**
Blyford. *Suff* —2D **27**
Blythburgh. *Suff* —2D **27**
Bobbingworth. *Essx* —3C **39**
Bocking. *Essx* —1A **40**
Bocking Churchstreet. *Essx*
—1A **40**
Bodham. *Norf* —1A **10**
Bodney. *Norf* —3B **16**
Bolnhurst. *Beds* —1B **28**
Boothby Pagnell. *Linc*
—2A **4**
Booton. *Norf* —3A **10**
Boreham. *Essx* —3A **40**
Borehamwood. *Herts*
—3C **37**
Borley. *Essx* —2B **32**
Borley Green. *Essx* —2B **32**
Borley Green. *Suff* —3C **25**
Boston. *Linc* —1A **6**
Botany Bay. *G Lon* —3D **37**

Botesdale. *Suff* —2D **25**
Botley. *Buck* —3A **36**
Bottisham. *Cambs* —3C **23**
Boughton. *Norf* —2D **15**
Bourn. *Cambs* —1A **30**
Bourne. *Linc* —3B **4**
Bourne End. *Beds* —2A **28**
Bourne End. *Beds*
(nr. Cranfield)
Bourne End. *Beds* —3B **20**
(nr. Sharnbrook)
Bourne End. *Herts* —3B **36**
Bovingdon. *Herts* —3B **36**
Bovinger. *Essx* —3C **39**
Bow Brickhill. *Mil* —3A **28**
Bowthorpe. *Norf* —2A **18**
Box End. *Beds* —2B **28**
Boxford. *Suff* —2C **33**
Boxted. *Essx* —3C **33**
Boxted. *Suff* —1B **32**
Boxted Cross. *Essx* —3C **33**
Boxworth. *Cambs* —3A **22**
Boxworth End. *Cambs*
—3A **22**
Boyden End. *Suff* —1A **32**
Boyton. *Suff* —2C **35**
Boyton Cross. *Essx* —3D **39**
Boyton End. *Essx* —3D **31**
Boyton End. *Suff* —2A **32**
Bozeat. *Nptn* —1A **28**
Brabling Green. *Suff* —3B **26**
Braceborough. *Linc* —1B **12**
Braceby. *Linc* —2B **4**
Bracon Ash. *Norf* —3A **18**
Bradfield. *Essx* —3A **34**
Bradfield. *Norf* —2B **10**
Bradfield Combust. *Suff*
—1B **32**
Bradfield Heath. *Essx*
—1A **42**
Bradfield St Clare. *Suff*
—1C **33**
Bradfield St George. *Suff*
—3C **25**
Bradwell. *Essx* —1B **40**
Bradwell. *Norf* —2D **19**
Bradwell-on-Sea. *Essx*
—3D **41**
Bradwell Waterside. *Essx*
—3C **41**
Bragbury End. *Herts* —1D **37**
Braintree. *Essx* —1A **40**
Braiseworth. *Suff* —2A **26**
Brakefield Green. *Norf*
—2D **17**
Bramerton. *Norf* —2B **18**
Bramfield. *Herts* —2D **37**
Bramfield. *Suff* —2C **27**
Bramford. *Suff* —2A **34**
Brampton. *Cambs* —2D **21**
Brampton. *Norf* —3B **10**
Brampton. *Suff* —1D **27**
Brancaster. *Norf* —1A **8**
Brancaster Staithe. *Norf*
—1A **8**
Brand End. *Linc* —1A **6**
Brandeston. *Suff* —3B **26**
Brandiston. *Norf* —3A **10**
Brandon. *Linc* —1A **4**
Brandon. *Suff* —1A **24**
Brandon Bank. *Cambs*
—1D **23**
Brandon Creek. *Norf* —3D **15**
Brandon Parva. *Norf* —2D **17**
Bran End. *Essx* —1D **39**
Brant Broughton. *Linc*
—1A **4**
Brantham. *Suff* —3A **34**

Braughing. *Herts* —1A **38**
Breachwood Green. *Herts*
—1C **37**
Breckles. *Norf* —3C **17**
Bredfield. *Suff* —1B **34**
Brent Eleigh. *Suff* —2C **33**
Brent Pelham. *Herts*
—3B **30**
Brentwood. *Essx* —3D **39**
Bressingham. *Norf* —1D **25**
Brettenham. *Norf* —1C **25**
Brettenham. *Suff* —1C **33**
Bricket Wood. *Herts*
—3C **37**
Bridge End. *Beds* —1B **28**
Bridge End. *Linc* —2C **5**
Bridge Green. *Essx* —3B **30**
Bridge Street. *Suff* —2B **32**
Bridgham. *Norf* —1C **25**
Briggate. *Norf* —3C **11**
Brightlingsea. *Essx* —2D **41**
Brightwell. *Suff* —2B **34**
Brigstock. *Nptn* —1A **20**
Bringhurst. *Leics* —3A **12**
Brington. *Cambs* —2B **20**
Briningham. *Norf* —2D **9**
Brinkley. *Cambs* —1D **31**
Brinton. *Norf* —2D **9**
Brisley. *Norf* —3C **9**
Briston. *Norf* —2D **9**
Broad Green. *Beds* —2A **28**
Broad Green. *Cambs*
—1D **31**
Broad Hill. *Cambs* —2C **23**
Broadley Common. *Essx*
—3B **38**
Broad's Green. *Essx* —2D **39**
Broad Street Green. *Essx*
—3B **40**
Broadway. *Suff* —2C **27**
Brockdish. *Norf* —2B **26**
Brockford Street. *Suff*
—3A **26**
Brockley. *Suff* —2B **24**
Brockley Green. *Suff* —2A **32**
(nr. Bury St Edmunds)
Brockley Green. *Suff* —1B **32**
(nr. Haverhill)
Brogborough. *Beds* —3A **28**
Brome. *Suff* —2A **26**
Brome Street. *Suff* —2A **26**
Bromeswell. *Suff* —1C **35**
Bromham. *Beds* —1B **28**
Bromley. *Herts* —1B **38**
Brooke. *Norf* —3B **18**
Brooke. *Rut* —2A **12**
Brookmans Park. *Herts*
—3D **37**
Brookville. *Norf* —3A **16**
Broom. *Beds* —2C **29**
Broome. *Norf* —3C **19**
Broomfield. *Essx* —2A **40**
Broom Green. *Norf* —3C **9**
Broomhill. *Norf* —2D **15**
Broomholm. *Norf* —2C **11**
Brotherhouse Bar. *Linc*
—1D **13**
Brothertoft. *Linc* —1D **5**
Broughton. *Cambs* —2D **21**
Broughton. *Mil* —3A **28**
Browston Green. *Norf*
—2D **19**
Broxbourne. *Herts* —3A **38**
Broxted. *Essx* —1C **39**
Bruisyard. *Suff* —3C **27**
Bruisyard Street. *Suff*
—3C **27**

Brundall. *Norf* —2C **19**
Brundish. *Norf* —3C **19**
Brundish. *Suff* —3B **26**
Brundish Street. *Suff*
—2B **26**
Bryant's Bottom. *Buck*
—3A **36**
Buckden. *Cambs* —3C **21**
Buckenham. *Norf* —2C **19**
Buckland. *Buck* —2A **36**
Buckland. *Herts* —3A **30**
Buckland Common. *Buck*
—3A **36**
Bucklegate. *Linc* —2A **6**
Bucklesham. *Suff* —2B **34**
Buckminster. *Leics* —3A **4**
Bucks Hill. *Herts* —3B **36**
Buckworth. *Cambs* —2C **21**
Bulbourne. *Herts* —2A **36**
Bulby. *Linc* —3B **4**
Bull's Green. *Herts* —2D **37**
Bulmer. *Essx* —2B **32**
Bulmer Tye. *Essx* —3B **32**
Bulwick. *Nptn* —3A **12**
Bumble's Green. *Essx*
—3B **38**
Bungay. *Suff* —1C **27**
Bunker's Hill. *Cambs*
—2B **14**
Bunker's Hill. *Suff* —2D **19**
Buntingford. *Herts* —1A **38**
Buntings Green. *Essx*
—3B **32**
Bunwell. *Norf* —3A **18**
Burcott. *Buck* —1A **36**
Bures. *Suff* —3C **33**
Burgate Great Green. *Suff*
—2D **25**
Burgate Little Green. *Suff*
—2D **25**
Burgh. *Suff* —1B **34**
Burgh Castle. *Norf* —2D **19**
Burgh next Aylsham. *Norf*
—3B **10**
Burgh St Margaret. *Norf*
—1D **19**
Burgh St Peter. *Norf* —3D **19**
Burley. *Rut* —1A **12**
Burnham Deepdale. *Norf*
—1B **8**
Burnham Green. *Herts*
—2D **37**
Burnham Market. *Norf*
—1B **8**
Burnham Norton. *Norf*
—1B **8**
Burnham-on-Crouch. *Essx*
—3C **41**
Burnham Overy Staithe. *Norf*
—1B **8**
Burnham Overy Town. *Norf*
—1B **8**
Burnham Thorpe. *Norf*
—1B **8**
Burnt Heath. *Essx* —1D **41**
Burntstalk. *Norf* —2A **8**
Burrough End. *Cambs*
—1D **31**
Burrough Green. *Cambs*
—1D **31**
Burstall. *Suff* —2D **33**
Burston. *Norf* —1A **26**
Burthorpe. *Suff* —3A **24**
Burtoft. *Linc* —2D **5**
Burton Coggles. *Linc* —3A **4**
Burton Corner. *Linc* —1A **6**
Burton End. *Cambs* —2D **31**

Burton End. *Essx* —1C **39**
Burton Latimer. *Nptn*
—2A **20**
Burton Pedwardine. *Linc*
—1C **5**
Burton's Green. *Essx*
—1B **40**
Burwell. *Cambs* —3C **23**
Bury. *Cambs* —1D **21**
Bury Green. *Herts* —1B **38**
Bury St Edmunds. *Suff*
—3B **24**
Bush Green. *Norf* —3D **17**
(nr. Attleborough)
Bush Green. *Norf* —1B **26**
(nr. Harleston)
Bush Green. *Suff* —1C **33**
Bushmead. *Beds* —3C **21**
Bushy Common. *Norf*
—1C **17**
Bustard Green. *Essx* —1D **39**
Butley. *Suff* —1C **35**
Butley High Corner. *Suff*
—2C **35**
Butterwick. *Linc* —1A **6**
Butt's Green. *Essx* —3A **40**
Buxhall. *Suff* —1D **33**
Buxton. *Norf* —3B **10**
Bygrave. *Herts* —3D **29**
Bythorn. *Cambs* —2B **20**

Caddington. *Beds* —2B **36**
Cadwell. *Herts* —3C **29**
Caister-on-Sea. *Norf* —1D **19**
Caister St Edmund. *Norf*
—2B **18**
Cake Street. *Suff* —2D **23**
Calais Street. *Suff* —2C **33**
Caldecote. *Cambs* —1A **30**
(nr. Cambridge)
Caldecote. *Cambs* —1C **21**
(nr. Peterborough)
Caldecote. *Herts* —3D **29**
Caldecott. *Nptn* —3A **20**
Caldecott. *Rut* —3A **12**
Calford Green. *Suff* —2D **31**
California. *Norf* —1D **19**
California. *Suff* —2A **34**
Calthorpe. *Norf* —2A **10**
Calthorpe Street. *Norf*
—3D **11**
Cambridge. *Cambs* —1B **30**
Cambridge Airport. *Cambs*
—1B **30**
Campsea Ashe. *Suff* —1C **35**
Camps End. *Cambs* —2D **31**
Campton. *Beds* —3C **29**
Candle Street. *Suff* —2D **25**
Cangate. *Norf* —3C **11**
Canham's Green. *Suff*
—3D **25**
Cantley. *Norf* —2C **19**
Capel Green. *Suff* —2C **35**
Capel St Andrew. *Suff*
—2C **35**
Capel St Mary. *Suff* —3D **33**
Carbrooke. *Norf* —2C **17**
Cardinal's Green. *Cambs*
—2D **31**
Cardington. *Beds* —2B **28**
Careby. *Linc* —1B **12**
Cargate Green. *Norf* —1C **19**
Carlby. *Linc* —1B **12**
Carleton Forehoe. *Norf*
—2D **17**
Carleton Rode. *Norf* —3A **18**

Carleton St Peter. *Norf*
—2C **19**
Carlton. *Beds* —1A **28**
Carlton. *Cambs* —1D **31**
Carlton. *Suff* —3C **27**
Carlton Colville. *Suff* —3D **19**
Carlton Scroop. *Linc* —1A **4**
Castle Acre. *Norf* —1B **16**
Castle Ashby. *Nptn* —1A **28**
Castle Bytham. *Linc* —1A **12**
Castle Camps. *Cambs*
—2D **31**
Castle Hedingham. *Essx*
—3A **32**
Castle Hill. *Suff* —2A **34**
Castle Rising. *Norf* —3D **7**
Caston. *Norf* —3C **17**
Castor. *Pet* —3C **13**
Catfield. *Norf* —1C **11**
Catfield Common. *Norf*
—3C **11**
Cattawade. *Suff* —3A **34**
Catton. *Norf* —1B **18**
Catworth. *Cambs* —2B **20**
Cavendish. *Suff* —2B **32**
Cavenham. *Suff* —3A **24**
Cawston. *Norf* —3A **10**
Cawthorpe. *Linc* —3B **4**
Caxton. *Cambs* —1A **30**
Caythorpe. *Linc* —1A **4**
Cess. *Norf* —1D **19**
Chadstone. *Nptn* —1A **28**
Chainbridge. *Cambs* —2B **14**
Chain Bridge. *Linc* —1A **6**
Chalk End. *Essx* —2D **39**
Chalton. *Beds* —1C **29**
(nr. Bedford)
Chalton. *Beds* —1B **36**
(nr. Luton)
Chandler's Cross. *Herts*
—3B **36**
Channel End. *Beds* —1C **29**
Chantry. *Suff* —2A **34**
Chapelbridge. *Cambs*
—3D **13**
Chapel End. *Beds* —2B **28**
Chapelgate. *Linc* —3B **6**
Chapel Hill. *Linc* —1D **5**
Chapmore End. *Herts*
—2A **38**
Chappel. *Essx* —1B **40**
Charles Tye. *Suff* —1D **33**
Charlton. *Herts* —1C **37**
Charsfield. *Suff* —1B **34**
Chartridge. *Buck* —3A **36**
Chatham Green. *Essx*
—2A **40**
Chatteris. *Cambs* —1A **22**
Chattisham. *Suff* —2D **33**
Chaulden. *Herts* —3B **36**
Chaul End. *Beds* —1B **36**
Chawston. *Beds* —1C **29**
Chedburgh. *Suff* —1A **32**
Cheddington. *Buck* —2A **36**
Chedgrave. *Norf* —3C **19**
Chediston. *Suff* —2C **27**
Chediston Green. *Suff*
—2C **27**
Chellington. *Beds* —1A **28**
Chelmondiston. *Suff* —3B **34**
Chelmsford. *Essx* —3A **40**
Chelsworth. *Suff* —2C **33**
Chelveston. *Nptn* —3A **20**
Chenies. *Buck* —3B **36**
Chequers Corner. *Norf*
—2B **14**
Cherry Green. *Herts* —1A **38**

Cherry Hinton. *Cambs*
—1B **30**
Chesham. *Buck* —3A **36**
Chesham Bois. *Buck* —3A **36**
Cheshunt. *Herts* —3A **38**
Chesterton. *Cambs* —3B **22**
(nr. Cambridge)
Chesterton. *Cambs* —3C **13**
(nr. Peterborough)
Chettisham. *Cambs* —1C **23**
Cheveley. *Cambs* —3D **23**
Chevington. *Suff* —1A **32**
Chicheley. *Mil* —2A **28**
Chickering. *Suff* —2B **26**
Chignall St James. *Essx*
—3D **39**
Chignall Smealy. *Essx*
—2D **39**
Childwick Green. *Herts*
—2C **37**
Chillesford. *Suff* —1C **35**
Chiltern Green. *Beds* —2C **37**
Chilton Street. *Suff* —2A **32**
Chimney Street. *Suff*
—2A **32**
Chippenham. *Cambs*
—3D **23**
Chipperfield. *Herts* —3B **36**
Chipping. *Herts* —3A **30**
Chipping Hill. *Essx* —2B **40**
Chipping Ongar. *Essx*
—3C **39**
Chiswell Green. *Herts*
—3C **37**
Chittering. *Cambs* —3B **22**
Cholesbury. *Buck* —3A **36**
Chrishall. *Essx* —3B **30**
Christchurch. *Cambs*
—3B **14**
Church End. *Beds* —1A **36**
(nr. Dunstable)
Church End. *Beds* —3C **29**
(nr. Stotfold)
Church End. *Beds* —3A **28**
(nr. Woburn)
Church End. *Cambs* —1B **30**
(nr. Cambridge)
Church End. *Cambs* —1D **21**
(nr. Sawtry)
Church End. *Cambs* —2A **22**
(nr. Willingham)
Church End. *Cambs* —2A **14**
(nr. Wisbech)
Church End. *Essx* —1A **40**
(nr. Braintree)
Churchend. *Essx* —1D **39**
(nr. Great Dunmow)
Church End. *Essx* —2C **31**
(nr. Saffron Walden)
Church End. *Linc* —2D **5**
Church End. *Norf* —1C **15**
Church Langley. *Essx*
—3B **38**
Church Street. *Suff* —1D **27**
Clacton-on-Sea. *Essx*
—2A **42**
Clapgate. *Herts* —1B **38**
Clapham. *Beds* —1B **28**
Clare. *Suff* —2A **32**
Clark's Hill. *Linc* —3A **6**
Clavering. *Essx* —3B **30**
Claxton. *Norf* —2C **19**
Clay Common. *Suff* —1D **27**
Claydon. *Suff* —1A **34**
Clay End. *Herts* —1A **38**
Clayhythe. *Cambs* —3C **23**
Clay Lake. *Linc* —3D **5**

Claypole. *Linc* —1A **4**
Clenchwarton. *Norf* —3C **7**
Cley next the Sea. *Norf*
—1D **9**
Clifton. *Beds* —3C **29**
Clifton Reynes. *Mil* —1A **28**
Cliftonville. *Norf* —2C **11**
Clint Green. *Norf* —1D **17**
Clippesby. *Norf* —1D **19**
Clippings Green. *Norf*
—1D **17**
Clipsham. *Rut* —1A **12**
Clophill. *Beds* —3B **28**
Clopton. *Nptn* —1B **20**
Clopton Corner. *Suff* —1B **34**
Clopton Green. *Suff* —1A **32**
Clothall. *Herts* —3D **29**
Coalhill. *Essx* —3A **40**
Coates. *Cambs* —3A **14**
Cockayne Hatley. *Beds*
—2D **29**
Cock Clarks. *Essx* —3B **40**
Cockernhoe. *Herts* —1C **37**
Cockfield. *Suff* —1C **33**
Cockfosters. *G Lon* —3D **37**
Cock Green. *Essx* —2D **39**
Cockley Cley. *Norf* —2A **16**
Cockthorpe. *Norf* —1C **9**
Coddenham. *Suff* —1A **34**
Coddenham Green. *Suff*
—1A **34**
Codicote. *Herts* —2D **37**
Coggeshall. *Essx* —1B **40**
Coggeshall Hamlet. *Essx*
—1B **40**
Colby. *Norf* —2B **10**
Colchester. *Essx* —1D **41**
Cold Brayfield. *Mil* —1A **28**
Coldfair Green. *Suff* —3D **27**
Coldham. *Cambs* —2B **14**
Cold Norton. *Essx* —3B **40**
Colegate End. *Norf* —1A **26**
Cole Green. *Herts* —2D **37**
Coleman Green. *Herts*
—2C **37**
Colesden. *Beds* —1C **29**
Colkirk. *Norf* —3C **9**
Colliers End. *Herts* —1A **38**
Collyweston. *Nptn* —2A **12**
Colmworth. *Beds* —1C **29**
Colne. *Cambs* —2A **22**
Colne Engaine. *Essx* —3B **32**
Colney. *Norf* —2A **18**
Colney Heath. *Herts* —3D **37**
Colney Street. *Herts* —3C **37**
Colsterworth. *Linc* —3A **4**
Coltishall. *Norf* —1B **18**
Colton. *Norf* —2A **18**
Comberton. *Cambs* —1A **30**
Combs. *Suff* —1D **33**
Combs Ford. *Suff* —1D **33**
Commercial End. *Cambs*
—3C **23**
Coney Weston. *Suff* —2C **25**
Congham. *Norf* —3A **8**
Conington. *Cambs* —3A **22**
(nr. Fenstanton)
Conington. *Cambs* —1C **21**
(nr. Sawtry)
Conyers Green. *Suff* —3B **24**
Cookley. *Suff* —2C **27**
Cooksmill Green. *Essx*
—3D **39**
Coopersale Common. *Essx*
—3B **38**
Coopersale Street. *Essx*
—3B **38**

Copalder Corner. *Cambs*
—3A **14**
Copdock. *Suff* —2A **34**
Copford. *Essx* —1C **41**
Copford Green. *Essx* —1C **41**
Cople. *Beds* —2C **29**
Coppingford. *Cambs* —1C **21**
Copthall Green. *Essx*
—3B **38**
Copy's Green. *Norf* —2C **9**
Corby. *Nptn* —1A **20**
Corby Glen. *Linc* —3B **4**
Cornish Hall End. *Essx*
—3D **31**
Corpusty. *Norf* —3A **10**
Corton. *Suff* —3D **19**
Costessey. *Norf* —1A **18**
Coston. *Leics* —3A **4**
Coston. *Norf* —2D **17**
Coton. *Cambs* —1B **30**
Cottenham. *Cambs* —3B **22**
Cottered. *Herts* —1A **38**
Cotterstock. *Nptn* —3B **12**
Cottesmore. *Rut* —1A **12**
Cottingham. *Nptn* —3A **12**
Cotton. *Suff* —3D **25**
Cotton End. *Beds* —2B **28**
Countess Cross. *Essx*
—3B **32**
Covehithe. *Suff* —1D **27**
Coveney. *Cambs* —1B **22**
Covington. *Cambs* —2B **20**
Cowbit. *Linc* —1D **13**
Cowlinge. *Suff* —1A **32**
Cox Common. *Suff* —1D **27**
Coxford. *Norf* —3B **8**
Crabgate. *Norf* —3D **9**
Crafton. *Buck* —2A **36**
Crane's Corner. *Norf* —1C **17**
Cranfield. *Beds* —2A **28**
Cranford St Andrew. *Nptn*
—2A **20**
Cranford St John. *Nptn*
—2A **20**
Cranley. *Suff* —2A **26**
Cranmer Green. *Suff*
—2D **25**
Cranmore. *Linc* —2C **13**
Cransford. *Suff* —3C **27**
Cranwell. *Linc* —1B **4**
Cranwich. *Norf* —3A **16**
Cranworth. *Norf* —2C **17**
Cratfield. *Suff* —2C **27**
Craymere Beck. *Norf* —2D **9**
Creeting St Mary. *Suff*
—1D **33**
Creeting St Peter. *Suff*
—1D **33**
Creeton. *Linc* —3B **4**
Cressing. *Essx* —1A **40**
Cretingham. *Suff* —3B **26**
Crews Hill. *G Lon* —3A **38**
Crimplesham. *Norf* —2D **15**
Cringleford. *Norf* —2A **18**
Crockleford Heath. *Essx*
—1D **41**
Cromer. *Herts* —1D **37**
Cromer. *Norf* —1B **10**
Crossdale Street. *Norf*
—2B **10**
Cross End. *Essx* —3B **32**
Cross Green. *Suff* —1B **32**
(nr. Cockfield)
Cross Green. *Suff* —1C **33**
(nr. Hitcham)
Cross Street. *Suff* —2A **26**

Crostwight. *Norf* —3C **11**
Crow End. *Cambs* —1A **30**
Crowfield. *Suff* —1A **34**
Crow Green. *Essx* —3C **39**
Crowland. *Linc* —1D **13**
Crowland. *Suff* —2D **25**
Crown Corner. *Suff* —2B **26**
Crownthorpe. *Norf* —2D **17**
Crowshill. *Norf* —2C **17**
Croxton. *Cambs* —3D **21**
Croxton. *Norf* —2C **9**
(nr. Fakenham)
Croxton. *Norf* —1B **24**
(nr. Thetford)
Croydon. *Cambs* —2A **30**
Cryers Hill. *Buck* —3A **36**
Cublington. *Buck* —1A **36**
Cuckoo Bridge. *Linc* —3D **5**
Cuffley. *Herts* —3A **38**
Culford. *Suff* —3B **24**
Culverthorpe. *Linc* —1B **4**
Cumberlow Green. *Herts*
—3A **30**
Cutlers Green. *Essx* —3C **31**

Daffy Green. *Norf* —2C **17**
Dagnall. *Buck* —2A **36**
Dalham. *Suff* —3A **24**
Dallinghoo. *Suff* —1B **34**
Damgate. *Norf* —2D **19**
(nr. Acle)
Damgate. *Norf* —1D **19**
(nr. Martham)
Dam Green. *Norf* —1D **25**
Danbury. *Essx* —3A **40**
Dane End. *Herts* —1A **38**
Darmsden. *Suff* —1D **33**
Darrow Green. *Norf* —1B **26**
Darsham. *Suff* —3D **27**
Dassels. *Herts* —1A **38**
Datchworth. *Herts* —2D **37**
Datchworth Green. *Herts*
—2D **37**
Dawsmere. *Linc* —2B **6**
Debach. *Suff* —1B **34**
Debden. *Essx* —3C **31**
Debden Green. *Essx* —3B **38**
(nr. Loughton)
Debden Green. *Essx* —3C **31**
(nr. Saffron Walden)
Debenham. *Suff* —3A **26**
Dedham. *Essx* —3D **33**
Dedham Heath. *Essx*
—3D **33**
Deene. *Nptn* —3A **12**
Deenethorpe. *Nptn* —3A **12**
Deeping Gate. *Pet* —2C **13**
Deeping St James. *Linc*
—2C **13**
Deeping St Nicholas. *Linc*
—1D **13**
Dell, The. *Suff* —3D **19**
Delvin End. *Essx* —3A **32**
Dembleby. *Linc* —2B **4**
Denford. *Nptn* —2A **20**
Dengie. *Essx* —3C **41**
Denham. *Suff* —3A **24**
(nr. Bury St Edmunds)
Denham. *Suff* —2A **26**
(nr. Eye)
Denham Street. *Suff* —2A **26**
Dennington. *Suff* —3B **26**
Denny End. *Cambs* —3B **22**
Denston. *Suff* —1A **32**
Denton. *Cambs* —1C **21**
Denton. *Linc* —2A **4**

Denton. *Norf* —1B **26**
Denton. *Nptn* —1A **28**
Denver. *Norf* —2D **15**
Deopham. *Norf* —2D **17**
Deopham Green. *Norf*
—3D **17**
Depden. *Suff* —1A **32**
Depden Green. *Suff* —1A **32**
Dereham. *Norf* —1C **17**
Dersingham. *Norf* —2D **7**
Dickleburgh. *Norf* —1A **26**
Diddington. *Cambs* —3C **21**
Digswell. *Herts* —2D **37**
Dilham. *Norf* —3C **11**
Dillington. *Cambs* —3C **21**
Diss. *Norf* —2A **26**
Ditchingham. *Norf* —3C **19**
Ditton Green. *Cambs*
—1D **31**
Docking. *Norf* —2A **8**
Doddinghurst. *Essx* —3C **39**
Doddington. *Cambs* —3A **14**
Doddshill. *Norf* —2A **8**
Dogsthorpe. *Pet* —2D **13**
Donington. *Linc* —2D **5**
Donington Eaudike. *Linc*
—2D **5**
Donington South Ing. *Linc*
—2D **5**
Dorking Tye. *Suff* —3C **33**
Dorrington. *Linc* —1B **4**
Dovercourt. *Essx* —3B **34**
Downfield. *Cambs* —2D **23**
Downham. *Essx* —3A **40**
Downham Market. *Norf*
—2D **15**
Dowsby. *Linc* —3C **5**
Dowsdale. *Linc* —1D **13**
Drabblegate. *Norf* —3B **10**
Drayton. *Linc* —2D **5**
Drayton. *Norf* —1A **18**
Drayton Beauchamp. *Buck*
—2A **36**
Drayton Parslow. *Buck*
—1A **36**
Drinkstone. *Suff* —3C **25**
Drinkstone Green. *Suff*
—3C **25**
Drury Square. *Norf* —1C **17**
Dry Doddington. *Linc* —1A **4**
Dry Drayton. *Cambs* —3A **22**
Duck End. *Essx* —1D **39**
Duddenhoe End. *Essx*
—3B **30**
Duddington. *Nptn* —2A **12**
Dullingham. *Cambs* —1D **31**
Dullingham Ley. *Cambs*
—1D **31**
Duloe. *Beds* —3C **21**
Dunsby. *Linc* —3C **5**
Dunsmore. *Buck* —3A **36**
Dunstable. *Beds* —1B **36**
Dunstall Green. *Suff* —3A **24**
Dunston. *Norf* —2B **18**
Dunton. *Beds* —2D **29**
Dunton. *Norf* —2B **8**
Dunton Patch. *Norf* —2B **8**
Dunwich. *Suff* —2D **27**
Duton Hill. *Essx* —1D **39**
Duxford. *Cambs* —2B **30**
Dyke. *Linc* —3C **5**

Eaglethorpe. *Nptn* —3B **12**
Earith. *Cambs* —2A **22**
Earlesfield. *Linc* —2A **4**
Earlham. *Norf* —2A **18**

Earls Barton. *Nptn* —3A **20**
Earls Colne. *Essx* —1B **40**
Earl's Green. *Suff* —3D **25**
Earl Soham. *Suff* —3B **26**
Earl Stonham. *Suff* —1A **34**
Earsham. *Norf* —1C **27**
Earsham Street. *Suff*
—2B **26**
East Barsham. *Norf* —2C **9**
East Beckham. *Norf* —1A **10**
East Bergholt. *Suff* —3D **33**
East Bliney. *Norf* —1C **17**
East Bradenham. *Norf*
—2C **17**
East Bridge. *Suff* —3D **27**
East Carleton. *Norf* —2A **18**
East End. *Cambs* —2A **22**
East End. *Herts* —1B **38**
East End. *Suff* —3A **34**
Eastgate. *Norf* —3A **10**
East Gores. *Essx* —1B **40**
East Hanningfield. *Essx*
—3A **40**
East Harling. *Norf* —1C **25**
East Hatley. *Cambs* —1D **29**
Easthaugh. *Norf* —1D **17**
East Heckingham. *Linc* —1C **5**
Easthorpe. *Essx* —1C **41**
East Hyde. *Beds* —2C **37**
East Lexham. *Norf* —1B **16**
East Mersea. *Essx* —2D **41**
Eastmoor. *Norf* —2A **16**
Easton. *Cambs* —2C **21**
Easton. *Linc* —3A **4**
Easton. *Norf* —1A **18**
Easton. *Suff* —1B **34**
Easton Maudit. *Nptn* —1A **28**
Easton on the Hill. *Nptn*
—2B **12**
East Perry. *Cambs* —3C **21**
East Raynham. *Norf* —3B **8**
Eastrea. *Cambs* —3D **13**
East Rudham. *Norf* —3B **8**
East Runton. *Norf* —1A **10**
East Ruston. *Norf* —3C **11**
East Somerton. *Norf* —1D **19**
East Tuddenham. *Norf*
—1D **17**
East Walton. *Norf* —1A **16**
Eastwick. *Herts* —2B **38**
East Winch. *Norf* —1D **15**
Eastwood End. *Cambs*
—3B **14**
Eaton. *Norf* —2D **7**
(nr. Heacham)
Eaton. *Norf* —2B **18**
(nr. Norwich)
Eaton Bray. *Beds* —1A **36**
Eaton Green. *Beds* —1A **36**
Eaton Socon. *Cambs*
—1C **29**
Eau Brink. *Norf* —1C **15**
Eccles on Sea. *Norf* —3D **11**
Eccles Road. *Norf* —3D **17**
Edenham. *Linc* —3B **4**
Edgefield. *Norf* —2D **9**
Edgefield Street. *Norf* —2D **9**
Edingthorpe. *Norf* —2C **11**
Edith Weston. *Rut* —2A **12**
Edlesborough. *Buck* —2A **36**
Edmondthorpe. *Leics*
—1A **12**
Edney Common. *Essx*
—3D **39**
Edwardstone. *Suff* —2C **33**
Edworth. *Beds* —2D **29**
Eggington. *Beds* —1A **36**

Egleton. *Rut* —2A **12**
Eight Ash Green. *Essx*
—1C **41**
Eldernell. *Cambs* —3A **14**
Elder Street. *Essx* —3C **31**
Elford Closes. *Cambs*
—2B **22**
Elkins Green. *Essx* —3D **39**
Ellenbrook. *Herts* —3D **37**
Ellingham. *Norf* —3C **19**
Ellington. *Cambs* —2C **21**
Ellington Thorpe. *Cambs*
—2C **21**
Ellough. *Suff* —1D **27**
Elm. *Cambs* —2B **14**
Elmdon. *Essx* —3B **30**
Elmsett. *Suff* —2D **33**
Elmstead. *Essx* —1D **41**
Elmstead Heath. *Essx*
—1D **41**
Elmstead Market. *Essx*
—1D **41**
Elmswell. *Suff* —3C **25**
Elsenham. *Essx* —1C **39**
Elsing. *Norf* —1D **17**
Elsthorpe. *Linc* —3B **4**
Elstow. *Beds* —2B **28**
Elsworth. *Cambs* —3A **22**
Eltisley. *Cambs* —1D **29**
Elton. *Cambs* —3B **12**
Elveden. *Suff* —2B **24**
Ely. *Cambs* —1C **23**
Emberton. *Mil* —2A **28**
Emneth. *Norf* —2B **14**
Emneth Hungate. *Norf*
—2C **15**
Empingham. *Rut* —2A **12**
Enfield. *G Lon* —3A **38**
Enfield Wash. *G Lon* —3A **38**
Epping. *Essx* —3B **38**
Epping Green. *Essx* —3B **38**
Epping Green. *Herts* —3D **37**
Epping Upland. *Essx* —3B **38**
Eriswell. *Suff* —2A **24**
Erpingham. *Norf* —2A **10**
Erwarton. *Suff* —3B **34**
Essendine. *Rut* —1B **12**
Essendon. *Herts* —3D **37**
Etling Green. *Norf* —1D **17**
Etton. *Pet* —2C **13**
Euston. *Suff* —2B **24**
Evedon. *Linc* —1B **4**
Eversholt. *Beds* —3A **28**
Everton. *Beds* —1D **29**
Ewerby. *Linc* —1C **5**
Exning. *Suff* —3D **23**
Exton. *Rut* —1A **12**
Eye. *Pet* —2D **13**
Eye. *Suff* —2A **26**
Eye Green. *Pet* —2D **13**
Eyeworth. *Beds* —2D **29**
Eyke. *Suff* —1C **35**
Eynesbury. *Cambs* —3C **21**

Fair Green. *Norf* —1D **15**
Fairstead. *Essx* —2A **40**
Fairstead. *Norf* —1D **15**
Fakenham. *Norf* —3C **9**
Falkenham. *Suff* —3B **34**
Fancott. *Beds* —1B **36**
Fanner's Green. *Essx*
—2D **39**
Farley Green. *Suff* —1A **32**
Farndish. *Beds* —3A **20**
Farnham. *Essx* —1B **38**
Farnham. *Suff* —3C **27**

Farnham Green. *Essx*
—1B **38**
Faulkbourne. *Essx* —2A **40**
Feering. *Essx* —1B **40**
Felbrigg. *Norf* —2B **10**
Felden. *Herts* —3B **36**
Felixstowe. *Suff* —3C **35**
Felixstowe Ferry. *Suff*
—3C **35**
Felmersham. *Beds* —1A **28**
Felmingham. *Norf* —3B **10**
Felsham. *Suff* —1C **33**
Felsted. *Essx* —1D **39**
Felthorpe. *Norf* —1A **18**
Feltwell. *Norf* —1A **24**
Fen Ditton. *Cambs* —3B **22**
Fen Drayton. *Cambs* —3A **22**
Fen End. *Linc* —3D **5**
Fenhouses. *Linc* —1D **5**
Fenny Stratford. *Mil* —3A **28**
Fenstanton. *Cambs* —3A **22**
Fen Street. *Norf* —3D **17**
Fenton. *Cambs* —2A **22**
Fenton. *Linc* —1A **4**
Ferry Hill. *Cambs* —1A **22**
Fersfield. *Norf* —1D **25**
Fiddlers Hamlet. *Essx*
—3B **38**
Field Dalling. *Norf* —2D **9**
Filby. *Norf* —1D **19**
Filgrave. *Mil* —2A **28**
Fincham. *Norf* —2D **15**
Finchingfield. *Essx* —3D **31**
Finedon. *Nptn* —2A **20**
Fingal Street. *Suff* —2B **26**
Fingringhoe. *Essx* —1D **41**
Finningham. *Suff* —3D **25**
Fishley. *Norf* —1D **19**
Fishtoft. *Linc* —1A **6**
Fishtoft Drove. *Linc* —1A **6**
Fitton End. *Cambs* —1B **14**
Flack's Green. *Essx* —2A **40**
Flamstead. *Herts* —2B **36**
Flaunden. *Herts* —3B **36**
Fleet. *Linc* —3A **6**
Fleet Hargate. *Linc* —3A **6**
Fleetville. *Herts* —3C **37**
Fleggburgh. *Norf* —1D **19**
Flempton. *Suff* —3B **24**
Flitcham. *Norf* —3A **8**
Flitton. *Beds* —3B **28**
Flitwick. *Beds* —3B **28**
Flixton. *Suff* —1C **27**
Flood's Ferry. *Cambs*
—3A **14**
Flordon. *Norf* —3A **18**
Flowton. *Suff* —2D **33**
Folkingham. *Linc* —2B **4**
Folksworth. *Cambs* —3C **13**
Folly, The. *Herts* —2C **37**
Ford End. *Essx* —2D **39**
Fordham. *Cambs* —2D **23**
Fordham. *Essx* —1C **41**
Fordham. *Norf* —3D **15**
Fordham Heath. *Essx*
—1C **41**
Ford Street. *Essx* —1C **41**
Forncett End. *Norf* —3A **18**
Forncett St Mary. *Norf*
—3A **18**
Forncett St Peter. *Norf*
—3A **18**
Fornham All Saints. *Suff*
—3B **24**
Fornham St Martin. *Suff*
—3B **24**
Forty Hill. *G Lon* —3A **38**

Forward Green. *Suff* —1D **33**
Fosdyke. *Linc* —2A **6**
Foster Street. *Essx* —3B **38**
Foston. *Linc* —1A **4**
Fotheringhay. *Nptn* —3B **12**
Foul Anchor. *Cambs* —1B **14**
Foulden. *Norf* —3A **16**
Foulsham. *Norf* —3D **9**
Four Ashes. *Suff* —2D **25**
Four Gotes. *Cambs* —1B **14**
Fowlmere. *Cambs* —2B **30**
Foxearth. *Essx* —2B **32**
Fox Hatch. *Essx* —3C **39**
Foxley. *Norf* —3D **9**
Fox Street. *Essx* —1D **41**
Foxton. *Cambs* —2B **30**
Framingham Earl. *Norf*
—2B **18**
Framingham Pigot. *Norf*
—2B **18**
Framlingham. *Suff* —3B **26**
Frampton. *Linc* —2A **6**
Frampton West End. *Linc*
—1D **5**
Framsden. *Suff* —1A **34**
Frankfort. *Norf* —3C **11**
Frating Green. *Essx* —1D **41**
Freckenham. *Suff* —2D **23**
Freethorpe. *Norf* —2D **19**
Freiston. *Linc* —1A **6**
Freiston Shore. *Linc* —1A **6**
Frenze. *Norf* —1A **26**
Fressingfield. *Suff* —2B **26**
Freston. *Suff* —3A **34**
Frettenham. *Norf* —1B **18**
Friday Bridge. *Cambs*
—2B **14**
Frieston. *Linc* —1A **4**
Fring. *Norf* —2A **8**
Frinton-on-Sea. *Essx*
—2B **42**
Friston. *Suff* —3D **27**
Frith Bank. *Linc* —1A **6**
Frithsden. *Herts* —3B **36**
Frithville. *Linc* —1A **6**
Fritton. *Norf* —2D **19**
(nr. Great Yarmouth)
Fritton. *Norf* —3B **18**
(nr. Long Stratton)
Frogmore. *Herts* —3C **37**
Frognall. *Linc* —1C **13**
Frogshall. *Norf* —2B **10**
Froxfield. *Beds* —3A **28**
Fryerning. *Essx* —3D **39**
Fulbeck. *Linc* —1A **4**
Fulbourn. *Cambs* —1C **31**
Fuller Street. *Essx* —2A **40**
Fulmodestone. *Norf* —2C **9**
Fulney. *Linc* —3D **5**
Fundenhall. *Norf* —3A **18**
Furneux Pelham. *Herts*
—1B **38**
Fyfield. *Essx* —3C **39**

Gainsborough. *Suff* —2A **34**
Gainsford End. *Essx* —3A **32**
Galleyend. *Essx* —3A **40**
Galleywood. *Essx* —3A **40**
Gamlingay. *Cambs* —1D **29**
Gamlingay Cinques. *Cambs*
—1D **29**
Gamlingay Great Heath.
Cambs —1D **29**
Garboldisham. *Norf* —1D **25**
Garnsgate. *Linc* —3B **6**
Garvestone. *Norf* —2D **17**

Garwick. *Linc* —1C **5**
Gasthorpe. *Norf* —1C **25**
Gateley. *Norf* —3C **9**
Gaultree. *Norf* —2B **14**
Gay Bowers. *Essx* —3A **40**
Gayhurst. *Mil* —2A **28**
Gayton. *Norf* —1A **16**
Gayton Thorpe. *Norf* —1A **16**
Gaywood. *Norf* —3D **7**
Gazeley. *Suff* —3A **24**
Gedding. *Suff* —1C **33**
Geddington. *Nptn* —1A **20**
Gedney. *Linc* —3B **6**
Gedney Broadgate. *Linc*
—3B **6**
Gedney Drove End. *Linc*
—3B **6**
Gedney Dyke. *Linc* —3B **6**
Gedney Hill. *Linc* —1A **14**
Geeston. *Rut* —2A **12**
Geldeston. *Norf* —3C **19**
Gelston. *Linc* —1A **4**
Gestingthorpe. *Essx* —3B **32**
Gibraltar. *Suff* —1A **34**
Gillingham. *Norf* —3D **19**
Gimingham. *Norf* —2B **10**
Gipping. *Suff* —3D **25**
Gipsey Bridge. *Linc* —1D **5**
Girton. *Cambs* —3B **22**
Gisleham. *Suff* —1D **27**
Gislingham. *Suff* —2D **25**
Gissing. *Norf* —1A **26**
Glandford. *Norf* —1D **9**
Glapthorn. *Nptn* —3B **12**
Glaston. *Rut* —2A **12**
Glatton. *Cambs* —1C **21**
Glemsford. *Suff* —2B **32**
Glinton. *Pet* —2C **13**
Goddard's Corner. *Suff*
—3B **26**
Godmanchester. *Cambs*
—2D **21**
Goff's Oak. *Herts* —3A **38**
Goldhanger. *Essx* —3C **41**
Gold Hill. *Norf* —3C **15**
Goldington. *Beds* —1B **28**
Gonerby Hill Foot. *Linc*
—2A **4**
Good Easter. *Essx* —2D **39**
Gooderstone. *Norf* —2A **16**
Gorefield. *Cambs* —1B **14**
Gorleston-on-Sea. *Norf*
—2D **19**
Gosbeck. *Suff* —1A **34**
Gosberton. *Linc* —2D **5**
Gosberton Clough. *Linc*
—3C **5**
Gosfield. *Essx* —1A **40**
Gosmore. *Herts* —1C **37**
Graby. *Linc* —3B **4**
Grafham. *Cambs* —3C **21**
Grafton Underwood. *Nptn*
—1A **20**
Grantchester. *Cambs*
—1B **30**
Grantham. *Linc* —2A **4**
Graveley. *Cambs* —3D **21**
Graveley. *Herts* —1D **37**
Great Abington. *Cambs*
—2C **31**
Great Addington. *Nptn*
—2A **20**
Great Amwell. *Herts* —3A **38**
Great Ashfield. *Suff* —3C **25**
Great Baddow. *Essx* —3A **40**
Great Bardfield. *Essx*
—3D **31**

Great Barford. *Beds* —1C **29**
Great Barton. *Suff* —3B **24**
Great Bealings. *Suff* —2B **34**
Great Bentley. *Essx* —1A **42**
Great Bircham. *Norf* —2A **8**
Great Blakenham. *Suff*
—1A **34**
Great Bradley. *Suff* —1D **31**
Great Braxted. *Essx* —2B **40**
Great Bricett. *Suff* —1D **33**
Great Brickhill. *Buck* —3A **28**
Great Bromley. *Essx* —1D **41**
Great Canfield. *Essx* —2C **39**
Great Casterton. *Rut* —2B **12**
Great Chesterford. *Essx*
—2C **31**
Great Chishill. *Cambs*
—3B **30**
Great Clacton. *Essx* —2A **42**
Great Cornard. *Suff* —2B **32**
Great Cressingham. *Norf*
—2B **16**
Great Doddington. *Nptn*
—3A **20**
Great Dunham. *Norf* —1B **16**
Great Dunmow. *Essx*
—1D **39**
Great Easton. *Essx* —1D **39**
Great Easton. *Leics* —3A **12**
Great Ellingham. *Norf*
—3D **17**
Great Eversden. *Cambs*
—1A **30**
Great Finborough. *Suff*
—1D **33**
Greatford. *Linc* —1B **12**
Great Fransham. *Norf*
—1B **16**
Great Gaddesden. *Herts*
—2B **36**
Great Gidding. *Cambs*
—1C **21**
Great Glemham. *Suff*
—3C **27**
Great Gonerby. *Linc* —2A **4**
Great Gransden. *Cambs*
—1D **29**
Great Green. *Norf* —1B **26**
Great Green. *Suff* —1C **33**
(nr. Lavenham)
Great Green. *Suff* —2A **26**
(nr. Palgrave)
Great Hale. *Linc* —1C **5**
Great Hallingbury. *Essx*
—2C **39**
Great Hampden. *Buck*
—3A **36**
Great Harrowden. *Nptn*
—2A **20**
Great Henny. *Essx* —3B **32**
Great Hockham. *Norf*
—3C **17**
Great Holland. *Essx* —2B **42**
Great Horkesley. *Essx*
—3C **33**
Great Hormead. *Herts*
—3B **30**
Great Kingshill. *Buck*
—3A **36**
Great Leighs. *Essx* —2A **40**
Great Linford. *Mil* —2A **28**
Great Livermere. *Suff*
—2B **24**
Great Maplestead. *Essx*
—3B **32**
Great Massingham. *Norf*
—3A **8**

Great Melton. *Norf* —2A **18**
Great Missenden. *Buck*
—3A **36**
Great Moulton. *Norf* —3A **18**
Great Munden. *Herts*
—1A **38**
Great Notley. *Essx* —1A **40**
Great Oakley. *Essx* —1A **42**
Great Oakley. *Nptn* —1A **20**
Great Offley. *Herts* —1C **37**
Great Oxney Green. *Essx*
—3D **39**
Great Parndon. *Essx* —3B **38**
Great Paxton. *Cambs*
—3D **21**
Great Plumstead. *Norf*
—1C **19**
Great Ponton. *Linc* —2A **4**
Great Raveley. *Cambs*
—1D **21**
Great Ryburgh. *Norf* —3C **9**
Great Saling. *Essx* —1D **39**
Great Sampford. *Essx*
—3D **31**
Great Saxham. *Suff* —3A **24**
Great Shelford. *Cambs*
—1B **30**
Great Snoring. *Norf* —2C **9**
Great Staughton. *Cambs*
—3C **21**
Great Stukeley. *Cambs*
—2D **21**
Great Tey. *Essx* —1B **40**
Great Thurlow. *Suff* —1D **31**
Great Totham North. *Essx*
—2B **40**
Great Totham South. *Essx*
—2B **40**
Great Waldingfield. *Suff*
—2C **33**
Great Walsingham. *Norf*
—2C **9**
Great Waltham. *Essx*
—2D **39**
Great Welnetham. *Suff*
—1B **32**
Great Wenham. *Suff* —3D **33**
Great Wigborough. *Essx*
—2C **41**
Great Wilbraham. *Cambs*
—1C **31**
Great Witchingham. *Norf*
—1A **18**
Great Wratting. *Suff* —2D **31**
Great Wymondley. *Herts*
—1D **37**
Great Yarmouth. *Norf*
—2D **19**
Great Yeldham. *Essx* —3A **32**
Green End. *Beds* —2B **28**
Green End. *Herts* —3A **30**
(nr. Buntingford)
Green End. *Herts* —1A **38**
(nr. Stevenage)
Greenfield. *Beds* —3B **28**
Greengate. *Norf* —1D **17**
Greensgate. *Norf* —1D **17**
Greenstead Green. *Essx*
—1B **40**
Greensted Green. *Essx*
—3C **39**
Green Street. *Herts* —3C **37**
Green Street. *Suff* —2A **26**
Greenstreet Green. *Suff*
—2D **33**
Green Tye. *Herts* —2B **38**
Greetham. *Rut* —1A **12**

Grendon. *Nptn* —3A **20**
Gresham. *Norf* —2A **10**
Gressenhall. *Norf* —1C **17**
Gretton. *Nptn* —3A **12**
Grimsthorpe. *Linc* —3B **4**
Grimston. *Norf* —3A **8**
Grimstone End. *Suff* —3C **25**
Griston. *Norf* —3C **17**
Gromford. *Suff* —1C **35**
Groton. *Suff* —2C **33**
Grundisburgh. *Suff* —1B **34**
Gubblecote. *Herts* —2A **36**
Guestwick. *Norf* —3D **9**
Guestwick Green. *Norf*
—3D **9**
Guilden Morden. *Cambs*
—2D **29**
Guist. *Norf* —3C **9**
Gulling Green. *Suff* —1B **32**
Gunby. *Linc* —3A **4**
Gunthorpe. *Norf* —2D **9**
Gunthorpe. *Pet* —2C **13**
Guthram Gowt. *Linc* —3C **5**
Guyhirn. *Cambs* —2B **14**
Guyhirn Gull. *Cambs*
—2A **14**
Guy's Head. *Linc* —3B **6**

Hacconby. *Linc* —3C **5**
Haceby. *Linc* —2B **4**
Hacheston. *Suff* —1C **35**
Hackford. *Norf* —2D **17**
Haddenham. *Cambs* —2B **22**
Haddenham End. *Cambs*
—2B **22**
Haddiscoe. *Norf* —3D **19**
Haddon. *Cambs* —3C **13**
Hadham Cross. *Herts*
—2B **38**
Hadham Ford. *Herts* —1B **38**
Hadleigh. *Suff* —2D **33**
Hadleigh Heath. *Suff* —2C **33**
Hadley Wood. *G Lon*
—3D **37**
Hadstock. *Essx* —2C **31**
Hailey. *Oxon* —2A **38**
Hail Weston. *Cambs* —3C **21**
Hainford. *Norf* —1B **18**
Hales. *Norf* —3C **19**
Halesgate. *Linc* —3A **6**
Halesworth. *Suff* —2C **27**
Hall End. *Beds* —2B **28**
Halley. *Herts* —2A **38**
Hall Green. *Norf* —1A **26**
Hall's Green. *Herts* —1D **37**
Halstead. *Essx* —1B **40**
Haltoft End. *Linc* —1A **6**
Halton. *Buck* —3A **36**
Halvergate. *Norf* —2D **19**
Hamerton. *Cambs* —2C **21**
Hammond Street. *Herts*
—3A **38**
Hamperden End. *Essx*
—3C **31**
Hamrow. *Norf* —3C **9**
Hanby. *Linc* —2B **4**
Hanscombe End. *Beds*
—3C **29**
Hanthorpe. *Linc* —3B **4**
Hanworth. *Norf* —2A **10**
Happisburgh. *Norf* —2C **11**
Happisburgh Common. *Norf*
—3C **11**
Hapton. *Norf* —3A **18**
Hardingham. *Norf* —2D **17**
Hardley Street. *Norf* —2C **19**

Hardmead. *Mil* —2A **28**
Hardwick. *Cambs* —1A **30**
Hardwick. *Norf* —1B **26**
Hardwick. *Nptn* —3A **20**
Hardy's Green. *Essx* —1C **41**
Hare Green. *Essx* —1D **41**
Hare Street. *Essx* —3B **38**
Hare Street. *Herts* —1A **38**
Hargate. *Norf* —3A **18**
Hargrave. *Nptn* —2B **20**
Hargrave. *Suff* —1A **32**
Harkstead. *Suff* —3A **34**
Harlaxton. *Linc* —2A **4**
Harleston. *Norf* —1B **26**
Harleston. *Suff* —3D **25**
Harling Road. *Norf* —1C **25**
Harlington. *Beds* —3B **28**
Harlow. *Essx* —3B **38**
Harlton. *Cambs* —1A **30**
Harmer Green. *Herts*
—2D **37**
Harpenden. *Herts* —2C **37**
Harpley. *Norf* —3A **8**
Harringworth. *Nptn* —3A **12**
Harrold. *Beds* —1A **28**
Harrowden. *Beds* —2B **28**
Harston. *Cambs* —1B **30**
Harston. *Leics* —2A **4**
Hartest. *Suff* —1B **32**
Hartford. *Cambs* —2D **21**
Hartford End. *Essx* —2D **39**
Harwich. *Essx* —3B **34**
Hasketon. *Suff* —1B **34**
Haslingfield. *Cambs* —1B **30**
Hassingham. *Norf* —2C **19**
Hastingwood. *Essx* —3B **38**
Hastoe. *Herts* —3A **36**
Hatch. *Beds* —2C **29**
Hatching Green. *Herts*
—2C **37**
Hatfield. *Herts* —3D **37**
Hatfield Broad Oak. *Essx*
—2C **39**
Hatfield Heath. *Essx* —2C **39**
Hatfield Hyde. *Herts* —2D **37**
Hatfield Peverel. *Essx*
—2A **40**
Hatley St George. *Cambs*
—1D **29**
Haughley. *Suff* —3D **25**
Haughley Green. *Suff*
—3D **25**
Haultwick. *Herts* —1A **38**
Hauxton. *Cambs* —1B **30**
Haven Bank. *Linc* —1D **5**
Haverhill. *Suff* —2D **31**
Haverscroft Street. *Norf*
—3D **17**
Hawes Green. *Norf* —3B **18**
Hawkedon. *Suff* —1A **32**
Hawstead. *Suff* —1B **32**
Hawthorpe. *Linc* —3B **4**
Hay Green. *Norf* —1C **15**
Haynes. *Beds* —2B **28**
Haynes West End. *Beds*
—2B **28**
Hay Street. *Herts* —1A **38**
Hazeleigh. *Essx* —3B **40**
Heacham. *Norf* —2D **7**
Heath and Reach. *Beds*
—1A **36**
Heath, The. *Norf* —3B **10**
(nr. Buxton)
Heath, The. *Norf* —3C **9**
(nr. Fakenham)
Heath, The. *Norf* —3A **10**
(nr. Heavingham)

Heathton. *Suff* —3A **34**
Hebing End. *Herts* —1A **38**
Heckfield Green. *Suff*
—2A **26**
Heckfordbridge. *Essx*
—1C **41**
Heckington. *Linc* —1C **5**
Hedenham. *Norf* —3C **19**
Helhoughton. *Norf* —3B **8**
Helions Bumpstead. *Essx*
—2D **31**
Hellesdon. *Norf* —1B **18**
Hellington. *Norf* —2C **19**
Helmingham. *Suff* —1A **34**
Helpringham. *Linc* —1C **5**
Helpston. *Pet* —2C **13**
Hemblington. *Norf* —1C **19**
Hemel Hempstead. *Herts*
—3B **36**
Hemingford Abbots. *Cambs*
—2D **21**
Hemingford Grey. *Cambs*
—2D **21**
Hemingstone. *Suff* —1A **34**
Hemington. *Nptn* —1B **20**
Hemley. *Suff* —2B **34**
Hempnall. *Norf* —3B **18**
Hempnall Green. *Norf*
—3B **18**
Hemp's Green. *Essx* —1C **41**
Hempstead. *Essx* —3D **31**
Hempstead. *Norf* —2A **10**
(nr. Holt)
Hempstead. *Norf* —3D **11**
(nr. Stalham)
Hempton. *Norf* —3C **9**
Hemsby. *Norf* —1D **19**
Hengrave. *Suff* —3B **24**
Henham. *Essx* —1C **39**
Henley. *Suff* —1A **34**
Henlow. *Beds* —3C **29**
Henny Street. *Essx* —3B **32**
Henstead. *Suff* —1D **27**
Hepworth. *Suff* —2C **25**
Herringfleet. *Suff* —3D **19**
Herringswell. *Suff* —3A **24**
Hertford. *Herts* —2A **38**
Hertford Heath. *Herts*
—2A **38**
Hertingfordbury. *Herts*
—2A **38**
Hessett. *Suff* —3C **25**
Hethersett. *Norf* —2A **18**
Heveningham. *Suff* —2C **27**
Hevingham. *Norf* —3A **10**
Hexton. *Herts* —3C **29**
Heybridge. *Essx* —3D **39**
(nr. Brentwood)
Heybridge. *Essx* —3B **40**
(nr. Maldon)
Heybridge Basin. *Essx*
—3B **40**
Heydon. *Cambs* —2B **30**
Heydon. *Norf* —3A **10**
Heydour. *Linc* —2B **4**
Hickling. *Norf* —3D **11**
Hickling Green. *Norf* —3D **11**
Hickling Heath. *Norf* —3D **11**
Higham. *Suff* —3D **33**
(nr. Ipswich)
Higham. *Suff* —3A **24**
(nr. Newmarket)
Higham Ferrers. *Nptn*
—3A **20**
Higham Gobion. *Beds*
—3C **29**
High Barnet. *G Lon* —3D **37**

High Beech. *Essx* —3B **38**
High Common. *Norf* —2C **17**
High Cross. *Herts* —2A **38**
High Easter. *Essx* —2D **39**
High Ferry. *Linc* —1A **6**
Highfields. *Cambs* —1A **30**
High Garrett. *Essx* —1A **40**
High Green. *Norf* —2A **18**
High Kelling. *Norf* —1A **10**
High Laver. *Essx* —3C **39**
High Ongar. *Essx* —3C **39**
High Roding. *Essx* —2D **39**
High Street. *Suff* —1D **35**
(nr. Aldeburgh)
High Street. *Suff* —1C **27**
(nr. Bungay)
High Street. *Suff* —2D **27**
(nr. Yoxford)
Highstreet Green. *Essx*
—3A **32**
High Street Green. *Suff*
—1D **33**
Hightown Green. *Suff*
—1C **33**
High Wych. *Herts* —2B **38**
Hilborough. *Norf* —2B **16**
Hildersham. *Cambs* —2C **31**
Hilgay. *Norf* —3D **15**
Hilldyke. *Linc* —1A **6**
Hill Green. *Essx* —3B **30**
Hillington. *Norf* —3A **8**
Hilton. *Cambs* —3D **21**
Hinderclay. *Suff* —2D **25**
Hindolveston. *Norf* —3D **9**
Hindringham. *Norf* —2C **9**
Hingham. *Norf* —2D **17**
Hintlesham. *Suff* —2D **33**
Hinwick. *Beds* —3A **20**
Hinxton. *Cambs* —2B **30**
Hinxworth. *Herts* —2D **29**
Histon. *Cambs* —3B **22**
Hitcham. *Suff* —1C **33**
Hitchin. *Herts* —1C **37**
Hobbles Green. *Suff* —1A **32**
Hobbs Cross. *Essx* —3B **38**
Hockering. *Norf* —1D **17**
Hockering Heath. *Norf*
—1D **17**
Hockliffe. *Beds* —1A **36**
Hockwold cum Wilton. *Norf*
—1A **24**
Hoddesdon. *Herts* —3A **38**
Hoe. *Norf* —1C **17**
Hoffleet Stow. *Linc* —2D **5**
Hoggard's Green. *Suff*
—1B **32**
Holbeach. *Linc* —3A **6**
Holbeach Bank. *Linc* —3A **6**
Holbeach Clough. *Linc*
—3A **6**
Holbeach Drove. *Linc*
—1A **14**
Holbeach Hurn. *Linc* —3A **6**
Holbeach St Johns. *Linc*
—1A **14**
Holbeach St Marks. *Linc*
—2A **6**
Holbeach St Matthew. *Linc*
—2B **6**
Holbrook. *Suff* —3A **34**
Holder's Green. *Essx*
—1D **39**
Holdingham. *Linc* —1B **4**
Holkham. *Norf* —1B **8**
Holland Fen. *Linc* —1D **5**
Holland-on-Sea. *Essx*
—2A **42**

Hollesley. *Suff* —2C **35**
Hollingdon. *Buck* —1A **36**
Holly End. *Norf* —2B **14**
Holme. *Cambs* —1C **21**
Holme Hale. *Norf* —2B **16**
Holme next the Sea. *Norf*
—1A **8**
Holmer Green. *Buck* —3A **36**
Holmsey Green. *Suff*
—2D **23**
Holt. *Norf* —2D **9**
Holton. *Suff* —2C **27**
Holton St Mary. *Suff* —3D **33**
Holtsmere End. *Herts*
—2B **36**
Holwell. *Herts* —3C **29**
Holyfield. *Essx* —3A **38**
Holywell. *Cambs* —2A **22**
Holywell Row. *Suff* —2A **24**
Homersfield. *Suff* —1B **26**
Honey Tye. *Suff* —3C **33**
Honing. *Norf* —3C **11**
Honingham. *Norf* —1A **18**
Honington. *Linc* —1A **4**
Honington. *Suff* —2C **25**
Hoo. *Suff* —1B **34**
Hook. *Cambs* —3B **14**
Hook's Cross. *Herts* —1D **37**
Hop Pole. *Linc* —1C **13**
Hopton. *Suff* —2C **25**
Hopton on Sea. *Norf*
—2D **19**
Horbling. *Linc* —2C **5**
Horham. *Suff* —2B **26**
Horkesley Heath. *Essx*
—1C **41**
Horning. *Norf* —1C **19**
Horningsea. *Cambs* —3B **22**
Horningtoft. *Norf* —3C **9**
Horringer. *Suff* —3B **24**
Horseheath. *Cambs* —2D **31**
Horseway. *Cambs* —1B **22**
Horsey. *Norf* —3D **11**
Horsford. *Norf* —1A **18**
Horsham St Faith. *Norf*
—1B **18**
Horsley Cross. *Essx* —1A **42**
Horsleycross Street. *Essx*
—1A **42**
Horstead. *Norf* —1B **18**
Horton. *Buck* —2A **36**
Hougham. *Linc* —1A **4**
Hough-on-the-Hill. *Linc*
—1A **4**
Houghton. *Cambs* —2D **21**
Houghton Conquest. *Beds*
—2B **28**
Houghton Regis. *Beds*
—1B **36**
Houghton St Giles. *Norf*
—2C **9**
Hounslow Green. *Essx*
—2D **39**
Hoveton. *Norf* —1C **19**
Howe. *Norf* —2B **18**
Howe Green. *Essx* —3A **40**
(nr. Chelmsford)
Howegreen. *Essx* —3B **40**
(nr. Maldon)
Howell. *Linc* —1C **5**
How End. *Beds* —2B **28**
Howe Street. *Essx* —2D **39**
(nr. Chelmsford)
Howe Street. *Essx* —3D **31**
(nr. Finchingfield)
How Hill. *Norf* —1C **19**
Howlett End. *Essx* —3C **31**

Hoxne. *Suff* —2A **26**
Hubbert's Bridge. *Linc*
—1D **5**
Hughenden Valley. *Buck*
—3A **36**
Hulcott. *Buck* —2A **36**
Hulver Street. *Suff* —1D **27**
Humby. *Linc* —2B **4**
Hundle Houses. *Linc* —1D **5**
Hundon. *Suff* —2A **32**
Hungerton. *Linc* —2A **4**
Hunsdon. *Herts* —2B **38**
Hunstanton. *Norf* —1D **7**
Hunston. *Suff* —3C **25**
Huntingdon. *Cambs* —2D **21**
Huntingfield. *Suff* —2C **27**
Hunton Bridge. *Herts*
—3B **36**
Hunt's Corner. *Norf* —1D **25**
Hunworth. *Norf* —2D **9**
Hurst Green. *Essx* —2D **41**
Husborne Crawley. *Beds*
—3A **28**
Hyde Heath. *Buck* —3A **36**

Ickburgh. *Norf* —3B **16**
Ickleford. *Herts* —3C **29**
Ickleton. *Cambs* —2B **30**
Icklingham. *Suff* —2A **24**
Ickwell. *Beds* —2C **29**
Iken. *Suff* —1D **35**
Ilketshall St Andrew. *Suff*
—1C **27**
Ilketshall St Lawrence. *Suff*
—1C **27**
Ilketshall St Margaret. *Suff*
—1C **27**
Illington. *Norf* —1C **25**
Impington. *Cambs* —3B **22**
Ingatestone. *Essx* —3D **39**
Ingham. *Norf* —3C **11**
Ingham. *Suff* —2B **24**
Ingham Corner. *Norf* —3C **11**
Ingleborough. *Norf* —1B **14**
Ingoldisthorpe. *Norf* —2D **7**
Ingoldsby. *Linc* —2B **4**
Ingthorpe. *Rut* —2A **12**
Ingworth. *Norf* —3A **10**
Intwood. *Norf* —2A **18**
Inworth. *Essx* —2B **40**
Ipswich. *Suff* —2A **34**
Irchester. *Nptn* —3A **20**
Irnham. *Linc* —3B **4**
Iron Bridge. *Cambs* —3B **14**
Irstead. *Norf* —3C **11**
Irthlingborough. *Nptn*
—2A **20**
Isham. *Nptn* —2A **20**
Isleham. *Cambs* —2D **23**
Islip. *Nptn* —2A **20**
Itteringham. *Norf* —2A **10**
Itteringham Common. *Norf*
—3A **10**
Ivinghoe. *Buck* —2A **36**
Ivinghoe Aston. *Buck*
—2A **36**
Ivy Todd. *Norf* —2B **16**
Ixworth. *Suff* —2C **25**
Ixworth Thorpe. *Suff*
—2C **25**

Jasper's Green. *Essx*
—1A **40**
Jaywick. *Essx* —2A **42**
Jockey End. *Herts* —2B **36**

Johnson's Street. *Norf*
—1C **19**
Jordan Green. *Norf* —3D **9**

Kedington. *Suff* —2A **32**
Keeley Grèen. *Beds* —2B **28**
Keisby. *Linc* —3B **4**
Kelby. *Linc* —1B **4**
Kelling. *Norf* —1D **9**
Kelsale. *Suff* —3C **27**
Kelshall. *Herts* —3A **30**
Kelvedon. *Essx* —2B **40**
Kelvedon Hatch. *Essx*
—3C **39**
Kempston. *Beds* —2B **28**
Kempston Hardwick. *Beds*
—2B **28**
Kennett. *Cambs* —3D **23**
Kenninghall. *Norf* —1D **25**
Kennyhill. *Suff* —2D **23**
Kensworth. *Beds* —2B **36**
Kensworth Common. *Beds*
—2B **36**
Kentford. *Suff* —3A **24**
Kenton. *Suff* —3A **26**
Kersey. *Suff* —2D **33**
Kesgrave. *Suff* —2B **34**
Kessingland. *Suff* —1D **27**
Kessingland Beach. *Suff*
—1D **27**
Keswick. *Norf* —2C **11**
(nr. North Walsham)
Keswick. *Norf* —2B **18**
(nr. Norwich)
Kettering. *Nptn* —2A **20**
Ketteringham. *Norf* —2A **18**
Kettlebaston. *Suff* —1C **33**
Kettleburgh. *Suff* —3B **26**
Kettlestone. *Norf* —2C **9**
Ketton. *Rut* —2A **12**
Keysoe. *Beds* —3B **20**
Keysoe Row. *Beds* —3B **20**
Keyston. *Cambs* —2B **20**
Kidd's Moor. *Norf* —2A **18**
Kimberley. *Norf* —2D **17**
Kimbolton. *Cambs* —3B **20**
Kimpton. *Herts* —2C **37**
Kingsash. *Buck* —3A **36**
King's Cliffe. *Nptn* —3B **12**
Kingshall Street. *Suff*
—3C **25**
Kings Langley. *Herts* —3B **36**
King's Lynn. *Norf* —1D **15**
Kings Ripton. *Cambs*
—2D **21**
Kingston. *Cambs* —1A **30**
King's Walden. *Herts*
—1C **37**
Kinsbourne Green. *Herts*
—2C **37**
Kirby Bedon. *Norf* —2B **18**
Kirby Cane. *Norf* —3C **19**
Kirby Cross. *Essx* —1B **42**
Kirby-le-Soken. *Essx*
—1B **42**
Kirby Row. *Norf* —3C **19**
Kirkby la Thorpe. *Linc*
—1C **5**
Kirkby Underwood. *Linc*
—3B **4**
Kirkley. *Suff* —3D **19**
Kirstead Green. *Norf* —3B **18**
Kirtling. *Cambs* —1D **31**
Kirtling Green. *Cambs*
—1D **31**
Kirton. *Linc* —2A **6**

Kirton. *Suff* —3B **34**
Kirton End. *Linc* —1D **5**
Kirton Holme. *Linc* —1D **5**
Knapton. *Norf* —2C **11**
Knapwell. *Cambs* —3A **22**
Knebworth. *Herts* —1D **37**
Kneesworth. *Cambs* —2A **30**
Knight's End. *Cambs*
—3B **14**
Knodishall. *Suff* —3D **27**
Knotting. *Beds* —3B **20**
Knotting Green. *Beds*
—3B **20**
Knuston. *Nptn* —3A **20**

Lackford. *Suff* —2A **24**
Lakenham. *Norf* —2B **18**
Lakenheath. *Suff* —1A **24**
Lakesend. *Norf* —3C **15**
Lamarsh. *Essx* —3B **32**
Lamas. *Norf* —3B **10**
Lamb Corner. *Essx* —3D **33**
Landbeach. *Cambs* —3B **22**
Langenhoe. *Essx* —2D **41**
Langford. *Beds* —2C **29**
Langford. *Essx* —3B **40**
Langham. *Norf* —1D **9**
Langham. *Rut* —1A **12**
Langham. *Suff* —3C **25**
Langley. *Essx* —3B **30**
Langley. *Herts* —1D **37**
Langleybury. *Herts* —3B **36**
Langley Green. *Norf* —2C **19**
Langley Street. *Norf* —2C **19**
Langrick. *Linc* —1D **5**
Langtoft. *Linc* —1C **13**
Larling. *Norf* —1C **25**
Latchford. *Herts* —1A **38**
Latchingdon. *Essx* —3B **40**
Lathbury. *Mil* —2A **28**
Latimer. *Buck* —3B **36**
Laughton. *Linc* —2B **4**
Lavendon. *Mil* —1A **28**
Lavenham. *Suff* —2C **33**
Lawford. *Essx* —3D **33**
Lawshall. *Suff* —1B **32**
Laxfield. *Suff* —2B **26**
Laxton. *Nptn* —3A **12**
Layer Breton. *Essx* —2C **41**
Layer-de-la-Haye. *Essx*
—1C **41**
Layer Marney. *Essx* —2C **41**
Leadenham. *Linc* —1A **4**
Leaden Roding. *Essx*
—2C **39**
Leagrave. *Lutn* —1B **36**
Leake Common Side. *Linc*
—1A **6**
Leake Fold Hill. *Linc* —1B **6**
Leake Hurn's End. *Linc*
—1B **6**
Leasingham. *Linc* —1B **4**
Leavenheath. *Suff* —3C **33**
Ledburn. *Buck* —1A **36**
Lee Clump. *Buck* —3A **36**
Lee, The. *Buck* —3A **36**
Leighton Bromswold. *Cambs*
—2C **21**
Leighton Buzzard. *Beds*
—1A **36**
Leiston. *Suff* —3D **27**
Lemsford. *Herts* —2D **37**
Lenton. *Linc* —2B **4**
Lenwade. *Norf* —1D **17**
Lessingham. *Norf* —3C **11**

Letchmore Heath. *Herts*
—3C **37**
Letchworth. *Herts* —3D **29**
Letheringham. *Suff* —1B **34**
Letheringsett. *Norf* —2D **9**
Letty Green. *Herts* —2D **37**
Levens Green. *Herts* —1A **38**
Leverington. *Cambs* —1B **14**
Leverton. *Linc* —1B **6**
Leverton Lucasgate. *Linc*
—1B **6**
Leverton Outgate. *Linc*
—1B **6**
Levington. *Suff* —3B **34**
Ley Green. *Herts* —1C **37**
Ley Hill. *Buck* —3A **36**
Leziate. *Norf* —1D **15**
Lidgate. *Suff* —1A **32**
Lidlington. *Beds* —3A **28**
Lilley. *Herts* —1C **37**
Limbury. *Lutn* —1B **36**
Limpenhoe. *Norf* —2C **19**
Lindsell. *Essx* —1D **39**
Lindsey. *Suff* —2C **33**
Lindsey Tye. *Suff* —2C **33**
Ling, The. *Norf* —3C **19**
Lingwood. *Norf* —2C **19**
Linslade. *Beds* —1A **36**
Linstead Parva. *Suff* —2C **27**
Linton. *Cambs* —2C **31**
Liston. *Essx* —2B **32**
Litcham. *Norf* —1B **16**
Litlington. *Cambs* —2A **30**
Little Abington. *Cambs*
—2C **31**
Little Addington. *Nptn*
—2A **20**
Little Baddow. *Essx* —3A **40**
Little Bardfield. *Essx* —3D **31**
Little Barford. *Beds* —1C **29**
Little Barningham. *Norf*
—2A **10**
Little Bealings. *Suff* —2B **34**
Little Bentley. *Essx* —1A **42**
Little Billington. *Beds*
—1A **36**
Little Blakenham. *Suff*
—2A **34**
Little Bradley. *Suff* —1D **31**
Little Brickhill. *Buck* —3A **28**
Little Bromley. *Essx* —1D **41**
Littlebury. *Essx* —3C **31**
Littlebury Green. *Essx*
—3B **30**
Little Bytham. *Linc* —1B **12**
Little Canfield. *Essx* —1C **39**
Little Casterton. *Rut* —2B **12**
Little Catworth. *Cambs*
—2C **21**
Little Chalfont. *Buck* —3A **36**
Little Chesterford. *Essx*
—2C **31**
Little Chishill. *Cambs*
—3B **30**
Little Clacton. *Essx* —2A **42**
Little Cornard. *Suff* —3B **32**
Little Crawley. *Mil* —2A **28**
Little Cressingham. *Norf*
—2B **16**
Little Ditton. *Cambs* —1D **31**
Little Downham. *Cambs*
—1C **23**
Little Dunham. *Norf* —1B **16**
Little Dunmow. *Essx* —1D **39**
Little Easton. *Essx* —1D **39**
Little Ellingham. *Norf*
—3D **17**

Little End. *Essx* —3C **39**
Little Eversden. *Cambs*
—1A **30**
Little Fakenham. *Suff*
—2C **25**
Little Fransham. *Norf*
—1C **17**
Little Gaddesden. *Herts*
—2A **36**
Little Gidding. *Cambs*
—1C **21**
Little Glemham. *Suff* —1C **35**
Little Gransden. *Cambs*
—1D **29**
Little Hadham. *Herts* —1B **38**
Little Hale. *Linc* —1C **5**
Little Hallingbury. *Essx*
—2B **38**
Little Hampden. *Buck*
—3A **36**
Little Harrowden. *Nptn*
—2A **20**
Little Hautbois. *Norf* —3B **10**
Little Horkesley. *Essx*
—3C **33**
Little Hormead. *Herts*
—1B **38**
Little Irchester. *Nptn* —3A **20**
Little Kingshill. *Buck*
—3A **36**
Little Laver. *Essx* —3C **39**
Little Leighs. *Essx* —2A **40**
Little Linford. *Mil* —2A **28**
Little London. *Linc* —3B **6**
(nr. Long Sutton)
Little London. *Linc* —3D **5**
(nr. Spalding)
Little London. *Norf* —2B **10**
(nr. North Walsham)
Little London. *Norf* —3A **16**
(nr. Northwold)
Little London. *Norf* —2A **10**
(nr. Saxthorpe)
Little London. *Norf* —3D **15**
(nr. Southery)
Little Maplestead. *Essx*
—3B **32**
Little Massingham. *Norf*
—3A **8**
Little Melton. *Norf* —2A **18**
Little Missenden. *Buck*
—3A **36**
Little Oakley. *Essx* —1B **42**
Little Oakley. *Nptn* —1A **20**
Little Ouse. *Norf* —1D **23**
Little Paxton. *Cambs*
—3C **21**
Little Plumstead. *Norf*
—1C **19**
Little Ponton. *Linc* —2A **4**
Littleport. *Cambs* —1C **23**
Little Raveley. *Cambs*
—2D **21**
Little Ryburgh. *Norf* —3C **9**
Little Sampford. *Essx*
—3D **31**
Little Saxham. *Suff* —3A **24**
Little Shelford. *Cambs*
—1B **30**
Little Snoring. *Norf* —2C **9**
Little Staughton. *Beds*
—3C **21**
Little Stonham. *Suff* —3A **26**
Little Street. *Cambs* —1C **23**
Little Stukeley. *Cambs*
—2D **21**
Little Sutton. *Linc* —3B **6**

Little Tey. *Essx* —1B **40**
Little Thetford. *Cambs*
—2C **23**
Little Thurlow. *Suff* —1D **31**
Little Totham. *Essx* —2B **40**
Little Walden. *Essx* —2C **31**
Little Waldingfield. *Suff*
—2C **33**
Little Walsingham. *Norf*
—2C **9**
Little Waltham. *Essx* —2A **40**
Little Welnetham. *Suff*
—1B **32**
Little Wenham. *Suff* —3D **33**
Little Whittingham Green.
Suff —2B **26**
Little Wilbraham. *Cambs*
—1C **31**
Little Wisbeach. *Linc* —2C **5**
Littleworth. *Beds* —2B **28**
Little Wratting. *Suff* —2D **31**
Little Wymington. *Nptn*
—3A **20**
Little Wymondley. *Herts*
—1D **37**
Little Yeldham. *Essx* —3A **32**
Littley Green. *Essx* —2D **39**
Loddon. *Norf* —3C **19**
Lode. *Cambs* —3C **23**
Lolworth. *Cambs* —3A **22**
London Colney. *Herts*
—3C **37**
London Luton Airport. *Beds*
—1C **37**
London Stansted Airport.
Essx —1C **39**
Londonthorpe. *Linc* —2A **4**
Long Gardens. *Essx* —3B **32**
Longham. *Norf* —1C **17**
Long Marston. *Herts*
—2A **36**
Long Meadow. *Cambs*
—3C **23**
Long Melford. *Suff* —2B **32**
Longstanton. *Cambs*
—3A **22**
Longstowe. *Cambs* —1A **30**
Long Stratton. *Norf* —3A **18**
Long Sutton. *Linc* —3B **6**
Longthorpe. *Pet* —3C **13**
Long Thurlow. *Suff* —3D **25**
Loosegate. *Linc* —3A **6**
Loughton. *Essx* —3B **38**
Lound. *Linc* —1B **12**
Lound. *Suff* —3D **19**
Loves Green. *Essx* —3D **39**
Lower Benefield. *Nptn*
—1A **20**
Lower Dean. *Beds* —3B **20**
Lower East Carleton. *Norf*
—2A **18**
Lower End. *Nptn* —3A **20**
Lower Gravenhurst. *Beds*
—3C **29**
Lower Green. *Essx* —3B **30**
Lower Green. *Norf* —2C **9**
Lower Holbrook. *Suff*
—3A **34**
Lower Layham. *Suff* —2D **33**
Lower Nazeing. *Essx*
—3A **38**
Lower Raydon. *Suff* —3D **33**
Lower Shelton. *Beds*
—2A **28**
Lower Stow Bedon. *Norf*
—3C **17**
Lower Street. *Norf* —2B **10**

Lower Sundon. *Beds*
—1B **36**
Lower Thurlton. *Norf*
—3D **19**
Lowestoft. *Suff* —3D **19**
Low Fulney. *Linc* —3D **5**
Lowick. *Nptn* —1A **20**
Low Street. *Norf* —2D **17**
Luddington in the Brook.
Nptn —1C **21**
Ludham. *Norf* —1C **19**
Luffenhall. *Herts* —1D **37**
Lundy Green. *Norf* —3B **18**
Luton. *Lutn* —1B **36**
Luton (London) Airport. *Beds*
—1C **37**
Lutton. *Linc* —3B **6**
Lutton. *Nptn* —1C **21**
Lutton Gowts. *Linc* —3B **6**
Lyddington. *Rut* —3A **12**
Lye Green. *Buck* —3A **36**
Lynch Green. *Norf* —2A **18**
Lyndon. *Rut* —2A **12**
Lyng. *Norf* —1D **17**
Lyngate. *Norf* —2B **10**
(nr. North Walsham)
Lyngate. *Norf* —3C **11**
(nr. Worstead)

Mackerye End. *Herts*
—2C **37**
Madingley. *Cambs* —3A **22**
Magdalen Laver. *Essx*
—3C **39**
Magpie Green. *Suff* —2D **25**
Maldon. *Essx* —3B **40**
Mallows Green. *Essx* —1B **38**
Manea. *Cambs* —1B **22**
Manningtree. *Essx* —3A **34**
Manthorpe. *Linc* —1B **12**
(nr. Bourne)
Manthorpe. *Linc* —2A **4**
(nr. Grantham)
Manton. *Rut* —2A **12**
Manuden. *Essx* —1B **38**
March. *Cambs* —3B **14**
Margaret Roding. *Essx*
—2C **39**
Margaretting. *Essx* —3D **39**
Margaretting Tye. *Essx*
—3D **39**
Marham. *Norf* —2A **16**
Marholm. *Pet* —2C **13**
Market Deeping. *Linc*
—1C **13**
Market Overton. *Rut* —1A **12**
Market Weston. *Suff* —2C **25**
Marks Tey. *Essx* —1C **41**
Markyate. *Herts* —2B **36**
Marlesford. *Suff* —1C **35**
Marlingford. *Norf* —2A **18**
Marshalswick. *Herts* —3C **37**
Marsham. *Norf* —3A **10**
Marsh Side. *Norf* —1A **8**
Marston. *Notts* —1A **4**
Marston Moretaine. *Beds*
—2A **28**
Marsworth. *Buck* —2A **36**
Martham. *Norf* —1D **19**
Martlesham. *Suff* —2B **34**
Martlesham Heath. *Suff*
—2B **34**
Mashbury. *Essx* —2D **39**
Matching. *Essx* —2C **39**
Matching Green. *Essx*
—2C **39**

Matching Tye. *Essx* —2C **39**
Matlaske. *Norf* —2A **10**
Mattishall. *Norf* —1D **17**
Mattishall Burgh. *Norf*
—1D **17**
Maulden. *Beds* —3B **28**
Mautby. *Norf* —1D **19**
Maxey. *Pet* —2C **13**
Mayland. *Essx* —3C **41**
Maylandsea. *Essx* —3C **41**
Maypole Green. *Norf*
—3D **19**
Maypole Green. *Suff* —1C **33**
Meesden. *Herts* —3B **36**
Meeting Green. *Suff* —1A **32**
Melbourn. *Cambs* —2A **30**
Melchbourne. *Beds* —3B **20**
Meldreth. *Cambs* —2A **30**
Mellis. *Suff* —2D **25**
Melton. *Suff* —1B **34**
Melton Constable. *Norf*
—2D **9**
Mendham. *Suff* —1B **26**
Mendlesham. *Suff* —3A **26**
Mendlesham Green. *Suff*
—3D **25**
Mentmore. *Buck* —2A **36**
Mepal. *Cambs* —1B **22**
Meppershall. *Beds* —3C **29**
Merton. *Norf* —3C **17**
Messing. *Essx* —2B **40**
Metfield. *Suff* —1B **26**
Methwold. *Norf* —3A **16**
Methwold Hythe. *Norf*
—3A **16**
Mettingham. *Suff* —3C **19**
Metton. *Norf* —2A **10**
Mickfield. *Suff* —3A **26**
Micklefield Green. *Herts*
—3B **36**
Mickley Green. *Suff* —1B **32**
Middle Harling. *Norf* —1C **25**
Middleton. *Essx* —3B **32**
Middleton. *Norf* —1D **15**
Middleton. *Nptn* —3A **20**
Middleton. *Suff* —3D **27**
Middlewood Green. *Suff*
—3D **25**
Milden. *Suff* —2C **33**
Mildenhall. *Suff* —2A **24**
Mile End. *Cambs* —1D **23**
Mile End. *Essx* —1C **41**
Mileham. *Norf* —1C **17**
Millbrook. *Beds* —3B **28**
Mill Common. *Suff* —1D **27**
Mill End. *Cambs* —1D **31**
Mill End. *Herts* —3A **30**
Millfield. *Pet* —3C **13**
Mill Green. *Norf* —1A **26**
Mill Green. *Suff* —2C **33**
Mill Greep. *Essx* —3D **39**
Millow. *Beds* —2D **29**
Mill Street. *Norf* —1D **17**
(nr. Lyng)
Mill Street. *Norf* —1D **17**
(nr. Swanton Morley)
Mill Street. *Suff* —2D **25**
Millthorpe. *Linc* —2C **5**
Milton. *Cambs* —3B **22**
Milton Bryan. *Beds* —3A **28**
Milton Ernest. *Beds* —1B **28**
Milton Keynes. *Mil* —3A **28**
Milton Keynes Village. *Mil*
—3A **28**
Mistley. *Essx* —3A **34**
Mistley Heath. *Essx* —3A **34**
Moats Tye. *Suff* —1D **33**

Mogerhanger. *Beds* —2C **29**
Molehill Green. *Essx* —1C **39**
Molesworth. *Cambs* —2B **20**
Monewden. *Suff* —1B **34**
Monken Hadley. *G Lon*
—3D **37**
Monks Eleigh. *Suff* —2C **33**
Monk Soham. *Suff* —3B **26**
Monk Soham Green. *Suff*
—3B **26**
Monk Street. *Essx* —1D **39**
Morborne. *Cambs* —3C **13**
Morcott. *Rut* —2A **12**
Morely St Botolph. *Norf*
—3D **17**
Moreton. *Essx* —3C **39**
Morningthorpe. *Norf* —3B **18**
Morris Green. *Essx* —3A **32**
Morston. *Norf* —1D **9**
Morton. *Linc* —3B **4**
Morton. *Norf* —1A **18**
Moulsoe. *Mil* —2A **28**
Moulton. *Linc* —3A **6**
Moulton. *Suff* —3D **23**
Moulton Chapel. *Linc*
—1D **13**
Moulton Eugate. *Linc*
—1D **13**
Moulton St Mary. *Norf*
—2C **19**
Moulton Seas End. *Linc*
—3A **6**
Mount Bures. *Essx* —3C **33**
Mountnessing. *Essx* —3D **39**
Mount Pleasant. *Norf*
—3C **17**
Much Hadham. *Herts*
—2B **38**
Muckleton. *Norf* —2B **8**
Mulbarton. *Norf* —2A **18**
Mundesley. *Norf* —2C **11**
Mundford. *Norf* —3B **16**
Mundham. *Norf* —3C **19**
Mundon. *Essx* —3B **40**
Murrow. *Cambs* —2A **14**
Mutford. *Suff* —1D **27**

Nacton. *Suff* —2B **34**
Naphill. *Buck* —3A **36**
Narborough. *Norf* —1A **16**
Nash Lee. *Buck* —3A **36**
Nassington. *Nptn* —3B **12**
Nasty. *Herts* —1A **38**
Naughton. *Suff* —2D **33**
Navestock Heath. *Essx*
—3C **39**
Navestock Side. *Essx*
—3C **39**
Nayland. *Suff* —3C **33**
Nazeing. *Essx* —3B **38**
Neatishead. *Norf* —3C **11**
Neaton. *Norf* —2C **17**
Necton. *Norf* —2B **16**
Nedging. *Suff* —2D **33**
Nedging Tye. *Suff* —2D **33**
Needham. *Norf* —1B **26**
Needham Market. *Suff*
—1D **33**
Needham Street. *Suff*
—3A **24**
Needingworth. *Cambs*
—2A **22**
Nene Terrace. *Linc* —2D **13**
Nethergate. *Norf* —3D **9**
Nether Street. *Essx* —2C **39**
Nettleden. *Herts* —2B **36**

Newark. *Pet* —2D **13**
Newborough. *Pet* —2D **13**
Newbourne. *Suff* —2B **34**
New Buckenham. *Norf*
—3D **17**
New Costessey. *Norf*
—1A **18**
New England. *Essx* —2A **32**
New England. *Pet* —2C **13**
Newgate. *Norf* —1D **9**
Newgate Street. *Herts*
—3A **38**
New Greens. *Herts* —3C **37**
New Hainford. *Norf* —1B **18**
New Holkham. *Norf* —2B **8**
New Houghton. *Norf* —3A **8**
Newman's Green. *Suff*
—2B **32**
Newmarket. *Suff* —3D **23**
New Mill. *Herts* —2A **36**
New Mistley. *Essx* —3A **34**
Newnham. *Cambs* —1B **30**
Newnham. *Herts* —3D **29**
Newport. *Essx* —3C **31**
Newport. *Norf* —1D **19**
Newport Pagnell. *Mil*
—2A **28**
New Rackheath. *Norf*
—1B **18**
Newton. *Cambs* —2B **30**
(nr. Cambridge)
Newton. *Cambs* —1B **14**
(nr. Wisbech)
Newton. *Linc* —2B **4**
Newton. *Norf* —1B **16**
Newton. *Nptn* —1A **20**
Newton. *Suff* —2C **33**
Newton Blossomville. *Mil*
—1A **28**
Newton Bromswold. *Nptn*
—3A **20**
Newton Flotman. *Norf*
—3B **18**
Newton Longville. *Buck*
—3A **28**
Newton St Faith. *Norf*
—1B **18**
Newtown. *Cambs* —3B **20**
New Town. *Lutn* —1B **36**
New Walsoken. *Cambs*
—2B **14**
New Wimpole. *Cambs*
—2A **30**
New World. *Cambs* —3A **14**
Nine Ashes. *Essx* —3C **39**
Nogdam End. *Norf* —2C **19**
Nordelph. *Norf* —2C **15**
Norman Cross. *Cambs*
—3C **13**
Normanton. *Linc* —1A **4**
North Acre. *Norf* —3C **17**
Northall. *Buck* —1A **36**
Northaw. *Herts* —3D **37**
North Barsham. *Norf* —2C **9**
Northbeck. *Linc* —1B **4**
Northborough. *Pet* —2C **13**
North Brook End. *Cambs*
—2D **29**
North Burlingham. *Norf*
—1C **19**
Northchurch. *Herts* —3A **36**
North Cove. *Suff* —1D **27**
North Crawley. *Mil* —2A **28**
North Creake. *Norf* —2B **8**
North Elmham. *Norf* —3C **9**
North End. *Essx* —2D **39**
(nr. Great Dunmow)

North End. *Essx* —3A **32**
(nr. Great Yeldham)
North End. *Linc* —1D **5**
North End. *Norf* —3C **17**
North Fambridge. *Essx*
—3B **40**
Northgate. *Linc* —3C **5**
North Green. *Norf* —1B **26**
North Green. *Suff* —3C **27**
(nr. Framlingham)
North Green. *Suff* —2C **27**
(nr. Halesworth)
North Green. *Suff* —3C **27**
(nr. Saxmundham)
Northill. *Beds* —2C **29**
North Kyme. *Linc* —1C **5**
Northlands. *Linc* —1A **6**
North Lopham. *Norf* —1D **25**
North Luffenham. *Rut*
—2A **12**
Northorpe. *Linc* —1B **12**
(nr. Bourne)
Northorpe. *Linc* —2D **5**
(nr. Donington)
North Pickenham. *Norf*
—2B **16**
North Rauceby. *Linc* —1B **4**
Northrepps. *Norf* —2B **10**
North Runcton. *Norf* —1D **15**
North Tuddenham. *Norf*
—1D **17**
North Walsham. *Norf*
—2B **10**
North Weald Bassett. *Essx*
—3C **39**
North Witham. *Linc* —3A **4**
Northwold. *Norf* —3A **16**
North Wootton. *Norf* —3D **7**
Norton. *Herts* —3D **29**
Norton. *Suff* —3C **25**
Norton Corner. *Norf* —3D **9**
Norton Heath. *Essx* —3D **39**
Norton Little Green. *Suff*
—3C **25**
Norton Mandeville. *Essx*
—3C **39**
Norton Subcourse. *Norf*
—3D **19**
Norwich. *Norf* —2B **18**
Norwich Airport. *Norf*
—1B **18**
Norwoodside. *Cambs*
—3B **14**
Nounsley. *Essx* —2A **40**
Nuthampstead. *Herts*
—3B **30**

Oakham. *Rut* —2A **12**
Oakington. *Cambs* —3B **22**
Oakley. *Beds* —1B **28**
Oakley. *Suff* —2A **26**
Oasby. *Linc* —2B **4**
Obthorpe. *Linc* —1B **12**
Occold. *Suff* —2A **26**
Odell. *Beds* —1A **28**
Odsey. *Cambs* —3D **29**
Offley Hoo. *Herts* —1C **37**
Offord Cluny. *Cambs*
—3D **21**
Offord D'Arcy. *Cambs*
—3D **21**
Offton. *Suff* —2D **33**
Old Buckenham. *Norf*
—3D **17**
Oldeamere. *Cambs* —3A **14**
Old Felixstowe. *Suff* —3C **35**

Old Fletton. *Pet* —3C **13**
Old Hall Street. *Norf* —2C **11**
Old Hunstanton. *Norf* —1D **5**
Old Hurst. *Cambs* —2D **21**
Old Knebworth. *Herts*
—1D **37**
Old Leake. *Linc* —1B **6**
Old Newton. *Suff* —3D **25**
Old Somerby. *Linc* —2A **4**
Old Warden. *Beds* —2C **29**
Old Weston. *Cambs* —2B **20**
Olmstead Green. *Cambs*
—2D **31**
Olney. *Mil* —1A **28**
Onehouse. *Suff* —1D **33**
Ongar Hill. *Norf* —3C **7**
Orford. *Suff* —2D **35**
Orlingbury. *Nptn* —2A **20**
Ormesby St Margaret. *Norf*
—1D **19**
Ormesby St Michael. *Norf*
—1D **19**
Orton Longueville. *Pet*
—3C **13**
Orton Waterville. *Pet*
—3C **13**
Orton Wistow. *Pet* —3C **13**
Orwell. *Cambs* —1A **30**
Osbournby. *Linc* —2B **4**
Ostend. *Essx* —3C **41**
Ostend. *Norf* —2C **11**
Otley. *Suff* —1B **34**
Oulton. *Norf* —3A **10**
Oulton. *Suff* —3D **19**
Oulton Broad. *Suff* —3D **19**
Oulton Street. *Norf* —3A **10**
Oundle. *Nptn* —1B **20**
Ousden. *Suff* —1A **32**
Outwell. *Norf* —2C **15**
Over. *Cambs* —2A **22**
Over End. *Cambs* —3B **12**
Overstrand. *Norf* —1B **10**
Ovington. *Essx* —2A **32**
Ovington. *Norf* —2C **17**
Oxborough. *Norf* —2A **16**
Oxen End. *Essx* —1D **39**
Oxley Green. *Essx* —2C **41**
Oxlode. *Cambs* —1B **22**
Oxwick. *Norf* —3C **9**

Pakefield. *Suff* —3D **19**
Pakenham. *Suff* —3C **25**
Palgrave. *Suff* —2A **26**
Pampisford. *Cambs* —2B **30**
Panfield. *Essx* —1A **40**
Panxworth. *Norf* —1C **19**
Papworth Everard. *Cambs*
—3D **21**
Papworth St Agnes. *Cambs*
—3D **21**
Parham. *Suff* —3C **27**
Parkeston. *Essx* —3B **34**
Park Street. *Herts* —3C **37**
Parsonage Green. *Essx*
—2A **40**
Parson Drove. *Cambs*
—2A **14**
Passingford Bridge. *Essx*
—3C **39**
Paston. *Norf* —2C **11**
Patchetts Green. *Herts*
—3C **37**
Patmore Heath. *Herts*
—1B **38**
Pattiswick. *Essx* —1B **40**
Pavenham. *Beds* —1A **28**

Peak Hill. *Linc* —1D **13**
Peakirk. *Pet* —2C **13**
Peaseland Green. *Norf*
—1D **17**
Peasenhall. *Suff* —3C **27**
Peats Corner. *Suff* —3A **26**
Pebmarsh. *Essx* —3B **32**
Pegsdon. *Beds* —3C **29**
Peldon. *Essx* —2C **41**
Pennygate. *Norf* —3C **11**
Penny Hill. *Linc* —3A **6**
Pentlow. *Essx* —2B **32**
Pentney. *Norf* —1A **16**
Perry Green. *Essx* —1B **40**
Perry Green. *Herts* —2B **38**
Pertenhall. *Beds* —3B **20**
Peterborough. *Pet* —3C **13**
Peter's Green. *Herts* —2C **37**
Petsoe End. *Mil* —2A **28**
Pettaugh. *Suff* —1A **34**
Pettistree. *Suff* —1B **34**
Pettywell. *Norf* —3D **9**
Piccadilly Corner. *Norf*
—1B **26**
Piccotts End. *Herts* —3B **36**
Pickworth. *Linc* —2B **4**
Pickworth. *Rut* —1A **12**
Pidley. *Cambs* —2A **22**
Pilgrims Hatch. *Essx*
—3C **39**
Pilsgate. *Pet* —2B **12**
Pilson Green. *Norf* —1C **19**
Pilton. *Nptn* —1B **20**
Pilton. *Rut* —2A **12**
Pinchbeck. *Linc* —3D **5**
Pinchbeck Bars. *Linc* —3C **5**
Pinchbeck West. *Linc* —3D **5**
Pinford End. *Suff* —1B **32**
Pin Mill. *Suff* —3B **34**
Pipewell. *Nptn* —1A **20**
Pirton. *Herts* —3C **29**
Pitstone. *Buck* —2A **36**
Pitstone Green. *Buck*
—2A **36**
Pixey Green. *Suff* —2B **26**
Playford. *Suff* —2B **34**
Pledgdon Green. *Essx*
—1C **39**
Pleshey. *Essx* —2D **39**
Plumstead. *Norf* —2A **10**
Pode Hole. *Linc* —3D **5**
Podington. *Beds* —3A **20**
Point Clear. *Essx* —2D **41**
Pointon. *Linc* —2C **5**
Polebrook. *Nptn* —1B **20**
Pollard Street. *Norf* —2C **11**
Polstead. *Suff* —3C **33**
Polstead Heath. *Suff* —2C **33**
Pondersbridge. *Cambs*
—3D **13**
Pond Street. *Essx* —3B **30**
Pool Street. *Essx* —3A **32**
Poringland. *Norf* —2B **18**
Porter's Fen Corner. *Norf*
—2C **15**
Poslingford. *Suff* —2A **32**
Postwick. *Norf* —2B **18**
Potsgrove. *Beds* —1A **36**
Potten End. *Herts* —3B **36**
Pottergate Street. *Norf*
—3A **18**
Potter Heigham. *Norf*
—1D **19**
Potters Bar. *Herts* —3D **37**
Potters Crouch. *Herts*
—3C **37**
Potter Street. *Essx* —3B **38**

Potthorpe. *Norf* —3C **9**
Potton. *Beds* —2D **29**
Pott Row. *Norf* —3A **8**
Poys Street. *Suff* —2C **27**
Poystreet Green. *Suff*
—1C **33**
Preston. *Herts* —1C **37**
Preston. *Rut* —2A **12**
Preston. *Suff* —1C **33**
Prestwood. *Buck* —3A **36**
Prickwillow. *Cambs* —1C **23**
Primrose Green. *Norf*
—1D **17**
Pristow Green. *Norf* —1A **26**
Puckeridge. *Herts* —1A **38**
Puddledock. *Norf* —3D **17**
Pulham Market. *Norf*
—1A **26**
Pulham St Mary. *Norf*
—1B **26**
Pulloxhill. *Beds* —3B **28**
Purleigh. *Essx* —3B **40**
Purl's Bridge. *Cambs*
—1B **22**
Puttenham. *Herts* —2A **36**
Puttock End. *Essx* —2B **32**
Puttock's End. *Essx* —2C **39**
Pye Corner. *Herts* —2B **38**
Pymore. *Cambs* —1B **22**
Pytchley. *Nptn* —2A **20**

Quadring. *Linc* —2D **5**
Quadring Eaudike. *Linc*
—2D **5**
Quarrington. *Linc* —1B **4**
Queen Adelaide. *Cambs*
—1C **23**
Quendon. *Essx* —3C **31**
Quidenham. *Norf* —1D **25**

Rableyheath. *Herts* —2D **37**
Rackheath. *Norf* —1B **18**
Radlett. *Herts* —3C **37**
Radwell. *Beds* —1B **28**
Radwell. *Herts* —3D **29**
Radwinter. *Essx* —3D **31**
Rampton. *Cambs* —3B **22**
Ramsden Heath. *Essx*
—3A **40**
Ramsey. *Cambs* —1D **21**
Ramsey. *Essx* —3B **34**
Ramsey Forty Foot. *Cambs*
—1A **22**
Ramsey Heights. *Cambs*
—1D **21**
Ramsey Island. *Essx*
—3C **41**
Ramsey Mereside. *Cambs*
—1D **21**
Ramsey St Mary's. *Cambs*
—1D **21**
Rank's Green. *Essx* —2A **40**
Ranworth. *Norf* —1C **19**
Rattlesden. *Suff* —1C **33**
Raunds. *Nptn* —2A **20**
Raveningham. *Norf* —3C **19**
Ravensden. *Beds* —1B **28**
Ravenstone. *Mil* —1A **28**
Raydon. *Suff* —3D **33**
Rayne. *Essx* —1A **40**
Reach. *Cambs* —3C **23**
Reading Green. *Suff* —2A **26**
Redbourn. *Herts* —2C **37**
Rede. *Suff* —1B **32**
Redenhall. *Norf* —1B **26**

Redgrave. *Suff* —2D **25**
Redhill. *Herts* —3D **29**
Redisham. *Suff* —1D **27**
Redlingfield. *Suff* —2A **26**
Red Lodge. *Suff* —2D **23**
Reed. *Herts* —3A **30**
Reed End. *Herts* —3A **30**
Reedham. *Norf* —2D **19**
Reepham. *Norf* —3D **9**
Rendham. *Suff* —3C **27**
Renhold. *Beds* —1B **28**
Repps. *Norf* —1D **19**
Rettendon. *Essx* —3A **40**
Reydon. *Suff* —2D **27**
Reymerston. *Norf* —2D **17**
Rickinghall Superior. *Suff*
—2D **25**
Rickling. *Essx* —3B **30**
Rickling Green. *Essx* —1C **39**
Ridge. *Herts* —3D **37**
Ridgewell. *Essx* —2A **32**
Ridgmont. *Beds* —3A **28**
Ridlington. *Norf* —2C **11**
Ridlington. *Rut* —2A **12**
Ringland. *Norf* —1A **18**
Ring's End. *Cambs* —2A **14**
Ringsfield. *Suff* —1D **27**
Ringsfield Corner. *Suff*
—1D **27**
Ringshall. *Buck* —2A **36**
Ringshall. *Suff* —1D **33**
Ringshall Stocks. *Suff*
—1D **33**
Ringstead. *Norf* —1A **8**
Ringstead. *Nptn* —2A **20**
Rippingale. *Linc* —3B **4**
Risby. *Suff* —3A **24**
Risegate. *Linc* —3D **5**
Riseley. *Beds* —3B **20**
Rishangles. *Suff* —3A **26**
Rivenhall. *Essx* —2B **40**
Rivenhall End. *Essx* —2B **40**
River Bank. *Cambs* —3C **23**
Road Green. *Norf* —3B **18**
Robinhood End. *Essx*
—3A **32**
Rockingham. *Nptn* —3A **12**
Rockland All Saints. *Norf*
—3C **17**
Rockland St Mary. *Norf*
—2C **19**
Rockland St Peter. *Norf*
—3C **17**
Roe Green. *Herts* —3A **30**
Rogue's Alley. *Cambs*
—2A **14**
Rollesby. *Norf* —1D **19**
Rooksey Green. *Suff* —1C **33**
Rootham's Green. *Beds*
—1C **29**
Ropsley. *Linc* —2A **4**
Rose Green. *Essx* —1B **40**
Rose Green. *Suff* —2C **33**
Rotten End. *Suff* —3C **27**
Rotten Row. *Norf* —1D **17**
Rougham. *Norf* —3B **8**
Rougham. *Suff* —3C **25**
Roughton. *Norf* —2B **10**
Roundbush Green. *Essx*
—2C **39**
Row Green. *Essx* —1A **40**
Row Heath. *Essx* —2A **42**
Rowhedge. *Essx* —1D **41**
Rowsham. *Buck* —2A **36**
Roxton. *Beds* —1C **29**
Roxwell. *Essx* —3D **39**
Roydon. *Essx* —2B **38**

Roydon. *Norf* —1D **25**
(nr. Diss)
Roydon. *Norf* —3A **8**
(nr. King's Lynn)
Roydon Hamlet. *Essx*
—3B **38**
Royston. *Herts* —2A **30**
Rucklers Lane. *Herts*
—3B **36**
Rudley Green. *Essx* —3B **40**
Rumburgh. *Suff* —1C **27**
Runcton Holme. *Norf*
—2D **15**
Runhall. *Norf* —2D **17**
Runham. *Norf* —1D **19**
Rushall. *Norf* —1A **26**
Rushbrooke. *Suff* —3B **24**
Rushden. *Herts* —3A **30**
Rushden. *Nptn* —3A **20**
Rushford. *Suff* —1C **25**
Rush Green. *Herts* —1D **37**
Rushmere. *Suff* —1D **27**
Rushmere St Andrew. *Suff*
—2A **34**
Rushton. *Nptn* —1A **20**
Ruskington. *Linc* —1B **4**
Russel's Green. *Suff* —2B **26**
Ryhall. *Rut* —1B **12**

Sacombe. *Herts* —2A **38**
Saddle Bow. *Norf* —1D **15**
Saffron Walden. *Essx*
—3C **31**
Saham Hills. *Norf* —2C **17**
Saham Toney. *Norf* —2B **16**
St Albans. *Herts* —3C **37**
St Clement. *Corn* —3C **7**
St Cross South Elmham. *Suff*
—1B **26**
St Ippollitts. *Herts* —1C **37**
St Ives. *Cambs* —2A **22**
St James South Elmham.
Suff —1C **27**
St John's Fen End. *Norf*
—1C **15**
St Lawrence. *Essx* —3C **41**
St Leonards. *Buck* —3A **36**
St Margaret's. *Herts* —3B **36**
(nr. Hemel Hempstead)
St Margarets. *Herts* —2A **38**
(nr. Hoddesdon)
St Margaret South Elmham.
Suff —1C **27**
St Michael South Elmham.
Suff —1C **27**
St Neots. *Cambs* —3C **21**
St Nicholas South Elmham.
Suff —1C **27**
St Olaves. *Norf* —3D **19**
St Osyth. *Essx* —2A **42**
St Osyth Heath. *Essx*
—2A **42**
St Paul's Walden. *Herts*
—1C **37**
Salcott. *Essx* —2C **41**
Salford. *Beds* —3A **28**
Salhouse. *Norf* —1C **19**
Salle. *Norf* —3A **10**
Salph End. *Beds* —1B **28**
Saltby. *Leics* —3A **4**
Salters Lode. *Norf* —2C **15**
Salthouse. *Norf* —1D **9**
Sandhill. *Cambs* —1C **23**
Sandholme. *Linc* —2A **6**
Sandon. *Essx* —3A **40**
Sandon. *Herts* —3A **30**

Sandridge. *Herts* —2C **37**
Sandringham. *Norf* —3D **7**
Sandy. *Beds* —2C **29**
Santon Downham. *Suff*
—1B **24**
Sapiston. *Suff* —2C **25**
Sapley. *Cambs* —2D **21**
Sapperton. *Linc* —2B **4**
Saracen's Head. *Linc* —3A **6**
Sarratt. *Herts* —3B **36**
Sawbridgeworth. *Herts*
—2B **38**
Sawston. *Cambs* —2B **30**
Sawtry. *Cambs* —1C **21**
Saxham Street. *Suff* —3D **25**
Saxlingham. *Norf* —2D **9**
Saxlingham Green. *Norf*
—3B **18**
Saxlingham Nethergate. *Norf*
—3B **18**
Saxlingham Thorpe. *Norf*
—3B **18**
Saxmundham. *Suff* —3C **27**
Saxon Street. *Cambs*
—1D **31**
Saxtead. *Suff* —3B **26**
Saxtead Green. *Suff* —3B **26**
Saxthorpe. *Norf* —2A **10**
Scarning. *Norf* —1C **17**
School Green. *Essx* —3A **32**
Scole. *Norf* —2A **26**
Sco Ruston. *Norf* —3B **10**
Scottlethorpe. *Linc* —3B **4**
Scottow. *Norf* —3B **10**
Scoulton. *Norf* —2C **17**
Scrane End. *Linc* —1A **6**
Scratby. *Norf* —1D **19**
Scredington. *Linc* —1B **4**
Sculthorpe. *Norf* —2B **8**
Seadyke. *Linc* —2A **6**
Sea Palling. *Norf* —3D **11**
Seaton. *Rut* —3A **12**
Seawick. *Essx* —2A **42**
Sedgebrook. *Linc* —2A **4**
Sedgeford. *Norf* —2A **8**
Seething. *Norf* —3C **19**
Semer. *Suff* —2D **33**
Setchey. *Norf* —1D **15**
Sewards End. *Essx* —3C **31**
Sewardstone. *Essx* —3A **38**
Sewell. *Beds* —1A **36**
Sewstern. *Leics* —3A **4**
Shadingfield. *Suff* —1D **27**
Shadwell. *Norf* —1C **25**
Shalford. *Essx* —1A **40**
Shalford Green. *Essx*
—1A **40**
Sharnbrook. *Beds* —1A **28**
Sharpenhoe. *Beds* —3B **28**
Sharp Street. *Norf* —3C **11**
Sharrington. *Norf* —2D **9**
Sheering. *Essx* —2C **39**
Shefford. *Beds* —3C **29**
Shelfanger. *Norf* —1A **26**
Shelley. *Suff* —3D **33**
Shellow Bowells. *Essx*
—3D **39**
Shelton. *Beds* —3B **20**
Shelton. *Norf* —3B **18**
Shelton Green. *Norf* —3B **18**
Shenley. *Herts* —3C **37**
Shenleybury. *Herts* —3C **37**
Shepeau Stow. *Linc* —1A **14**
Shephall. *Herts* —1D **37**
Shepherds Gate. *Norf*
—1C **15**
Shepherd's Port. *Norf* —2D **7**

Shepreth. *Cambs* —2A **30**
Shereford. *Norf* —3B **8**
Sheringham. *Norf* —1A **10**
Sherington. *Mil* —2A **28**
Shernborne. *Norf* —2A **8**
Shillington. *Beds* —3C **29**
Shimpling. *Norf* —1A **26**
Shimpling. *Suff* —1B **32**
Shimpling Street. *Suff*
—1B **32**
Shingay. *Cambs* —2A **30**
Shingham. *Norf* —2A **16**
Shingle Street. *Suff* —2C **35**
Shipdham. *Norf* —2C **17**
Shipmeadow. *Suff* —3C **19**
Shop Street. *Suff* —3B **26**
Short Green. *Norf* —1D **25**
Shortstown. *Beds* —2B **28**
Shotesham. *Norf* —3B **18**
Shotley. *Suff* —3B **34**
Shotley Gate. *Suff* —3B **34**
Shottisham. *Suff* —2C **35**
Shouldham. *Norf* —2D **15**
Shouldham Thorpe. *Norf*
—2D **15**
Shropham. *Norf* —3C **17**
Shrub End. *Essx* —1C **41**
Shudy Camps. *Cambs*
—2D **31**
Sible Hedingham. *Essx*
—3A **32**
Sibsey. *Linc* —1A **6**
Sibsey Fen Side. *Linc* —1A **6**
Sibson. *Cambs* —3B **12**
Sibton. *Suff* —3C **27**
Sicklesmere. *Suff* —3B **24**
Sidestrand. *Norf* —2B **10**
Silfield. *Norf* —3A **18**
Silk Willoughby. *Linc* —1B **4**
Silsoe. *Beds* —3B **28**
Silver End. *Essx* —2B **40**
Silvergate. *Norf* —3A **10**
Silverley's Green. *Suff*
—2B **26**
Six Mile Bottom. *Cambs*
—1C **31**
Sizewell. *Suff* —3D **27**
Skeldyke. *Linc* —2A **6**
Skeyton. *Norf* —3B **10**
Skeyton Corner. *Norf*
—3B **10**
Skillington. *Linc* —3A **4**
Skirbeck. *Linc* —1A **6**
Skirbeck Quarter. *Linc*
—1A **6**
Skye Green. *Essx* —1B **40**
Slade Field. *Cambs* —1A **22**
Slapton. *Buck* —1A **36**
Sleaford. *Linc* —1B **4**
Slip End. *Herts* —2B **36**
Slipton. *Nptn* —2A **20**
Sloley. *Norf* —3B **10**
Smallburgh. *Norf* —3C **11**
Smallworth. *Norf* —1D **25**
Smeeth, The. *Norf* —1C **15**
Smith's Green. *Essx* —1C **39**
Smithwood Green. *Suff*
—1C **33**
Smyth's Green. *Essx* —2C **41**
Snailwell. *Cambs* —3D **23**
Snape. *Suff* —1C **35**
Snetterton. *Norf* —3C **17**
Snettisham. *Norf* —2D **7**
Snow Street. *Norf* —1D **25**
Soham. *Cambs* —2C **23**
Soham Cotes. *Cambs*
—2C **23**

Somerleyton. *Suff* —3D **19**
Somersham. *Cambs* —2A **22**
Somersham. *Suff* —2D **33**
Somerton. *Suff* —1B **32**
Sotterley. *Suff* —1D **27**
Soulbury. *Buck* —1A **36**
Souldrop. *Beds* —3A **20**
South Acre. *Norf* —1B **16**
Southburgh. *Norf* —2C **17**
South Burlingham. *Norf*
—2C **19**
South Cove. *Suff* —1D **27**
South Creake. *Norf* —2B **8**
Southery. *Norf* —3D **15**
Southey Green. *Essx*
—3A **32**
Southgate. *Norf* —3A **10**
(nr. Aylsham)
Southgate. *Norf* —2D **7**
(nr. Dersingham)
Southgate. *Norf* —2B **8**
(nr. Fakenham)
South Green. *Essx* —2D **41**
South Hanningfield. *Essx*
—3A **40**
South Heath. *Buck* —3A **36**
South Heath. *Essx* —2A **42**
Southill. *Beds* —2C **29**
South Kyme. *Linc* —1C **5**
South Lopham. *Norf* —1D **25**
South Luffenham. *Rut*
—2A **12**
South Mimms. *Herts*
—3D **37**
Southminster. *Essx* —3C **41**
Southoe. *Cambs* —3C **21**
Southolt. *Suff* —3A **26**
Southorpe. *Pet* —2B **12**
South Pickenham. *Norf*
—2B **16**
South Rauceby. *Linc* —1A **4**
South Raynham. *Norf* —3B **8**
Southrepps. *Norf* —2B **10**
South Runcton. *Norf*
—2D **15**
Southtown. *Norf* —2D **19**
South Walsham. *Norf*
—1C **19**
Southwick. *Nptn* —3B **12**
South Witham. *Linc* —1A **12**
Southwold. *Suff* —2D **27**
Southwood. *Norf* —2C **19**
South Woodham Ferrers.
Essx —3B **40**
South Wootton. *Norf* —3D **7**
Sowley Green. *Suff* —1A **32**
Spa Common. *Norf* —2B **10**
Spalding. *Linc* —3D **5**
Spaldwick. *Cambs* —2C **21**
Spanby. *Linc* —2B **4**
Sparham. *Norf* —1D **17**
Sparhamhill. *Norf* —1D **17**
Sparrow Green. *Norf*
—1C **17**
Speen. *Buck* —3A **36**
Spellbrook. *Herts* —2B **38**
Spexhall. *Suff* —1C **27**
Spixworth. *Norf* —1B **18**
Spooner Row. *Norf* —3D **17**
Sporle. *Norf* —1B **16**
Sproughton. *Suff* —2A **34**
Sprowston. *Norf* —1B **18**
Sproxton. *Leics* —3A **4**
Stacksford. *Norf* —3D **17**
Stagden Cross. *Essx*
—2D **39**
Stagsden. *Beds* —2A **28**

Stainby. *Linc* —3A **4**
Stainfield. *Linc* —3B **4**
Stalham. *Norf* —3C **11**
Stalham Green. *Norf* —3C **11**
Stambourne. *Essx* —3A **32**
Stamford. *Linc* —2B **12**
Stanborough. *Herts* —2D **37**
Stanbridge. *Beds* —1A **36**
Standon. *Herts* —1A **38**
Standon Green End. *Herts*
—2A **38**
Standwell Green. *Suff*
—2A **26**
Stanfield. *Norf* —3C **9**
Stanford. *Beds* —2C **29**
Stanford Rivers. *Essx*
—3C **39**
Stanground. *Pet* —3D **13**
Stanhoe. *Norf* —2B **8**
Stanion. *Nptn* —1A **20**
Stanningfield. *Suff* —1B **32**
Stansfield. *Suff* —1A **32**
Stanstead. *Suff* —2B **32**
Stanstead Abbots. *Herts*
—2A **38**
Stansted (London) Airport.
Essx —1C **39**
Stansted Mountfitchet. *Essx*
—1C **39**
Stanton. *Suff* —2C **25**
Stanton Chare. *Suff* —2C **25**
Stanton Street. *Suff* —3C **25**
Stanway. *Essx* —1C **41**
Stanwick. *Nptn* —2A **20**
Stapleford. *Cambs* —1B **30**
Stapleford. *Herts* —2A **38**
Stapleford Tawney. *Essx*
—3C **39**
Staploe. *Beds* —3C **21**
Starling's Green. *Essx*
—3B **30**
Starston. *Norf* —1B **26**
Start Hill. *Essx* —1C **39**
Staughton Green. *Cambs*
—3C **21**
Staughton Highway. *Cambs*
—3C **21**
Stebbing. *Essx* —1D **39**
Stebbing Green. *Essx*
—1D **39**
Steeple. *Essx* —3C **41**
Steeple Bumpstead. *Essx*
—2D **31**
Steeple Gidding. *Cambs*
—1C **21**
Steeple Morden. *Cambs*
—2D **29**
Steppingley. *Beds* —3B **28**
Sternfield. *Suff* —3C **27**
Stetchworth. *Cambs* —1D **31**
Stevenage. *Herts* —1D **37**
Stevington. *Beds* —1A **28**
Stevington End. *Cambs*
—2C **31**
Stewartby. *Beds* —2B **28**
Stewkley. *Buck* —1A **36**
Stibbard. *Norf* —3C **9**
Stibbington. *Pet* —3B **12**
Stickling Green. *Essx*
—3B **30**
Stiffkey. *Norf* —1C **9**
Stilton. *Cambs* —1C **21**
Stisted. *Essx* —1A **40**
Stock. *Essx* —3D **39**
Stockerston. *Leics* —3A **12**
Stocking Green. *Essx*
—3C **31**

Stocking Pelham. *Herts*
—1B **38**
Stockstreet. *Essx* —1B **40**
Stockton. *Norf* —3C **19**
Stody. *Norf* —2D **9**
Stoke Ash. *Suff* —2A **26**
Stoke by Clare. *Suff* —2A **32**
Stoke-by-Nayland. *Suff*
—3C **33**
Stoke Doyle. *Nptn* —1B **20**
Stoke Dry. *Rut* —3A **12**
Stoke Ferry. *Norf* —3A **16**
Stoke Goldington. *Mil*
—2A **28**
Stoke Hammond. *Buck*
—1A **36**
Stoke Holy Cross. *Norf*
—2B **18**
Stoke Rochford. *Linc* —3A **4**
Stokesby. *Norf* —1D **19**
Stondon Massey. *Essx*
—3C **39**
Stonea. *Cambs* —3B **14**
Stone Bridge Corner. *Pet*
—2D **13**
Stonely. *Cambs* —3C **21**
Stones Green. *Essx* —1A **42**
Stone Street. *Suff* —3C **33**
(nr. Boxford)
Stone Street. *Suff* —1C **27**
(nr. Halesworth)
Stoneyhills. *Essx* —3C **41**
Stonham Aspal. *Suff* —1A **34**
Stopsley. *Lutn* —1C **37**
Stotfold. *Beds* —3D **29**
Stoven. *Suff* —1D **27**
Stow. *Linc* —2B **4**
Stow Bardolph. *Norf* —2D **15**
Stow Bedon. *Norf* —3C **17**
Stowbridge. *Norf* —2D **15**
Stow cum Quy. *Cambs*
—3C **23**
Stowlangtoft. *Suff* —3C **25**
Stow Longa. *Cambs* —2C **21**
Stow Maries. *Essx* —3B **40**
Stowmarket. *Suff* —1D **33**
Stowupland. *Suff* —1D **33**
Stradbroke. *Suff* —2B **26**
Stradishall. *Suff* —1A **32**
Stradsett. *Norf* —2D **15**
Stragglethorpe. *Linc* —1A **4**
Stratford St Andrew. *Suff*
—3C **27**
Stratford St Mary. *Suff*
—3D **33**
Stratton St Michael. *Norf*
—3B **18**
Stratton Strawless. *Norf*
—3B **10**
Streatley. *Beds* —1B **36**
Streetly End. *Cambs* —2D **31**
Strethall. *Essx* —3B **30**
Stretham. *Cambs* —2C **23**
Stretton. *Rut* —1A **12**
Strixton. *Nptn* —3A **20**
Stroxton. *Linc* —2A **4**
Strugg's Hill. *Linc* —2D **5**
Strumpshaw. *Norf* —2C **19**
Stubbs Green. *Norf* —3C **19**
Stubton. *Linc* —1A **4**
Studham. *Beds* —2B **36**
Stuntney. *Cambs* —2C **23**
Sturmer. *Essx* —2D **31**
Stuston. *Suff* —2A **26**
Stutton. *Suff* —3A **34**
Sudborough. *Nptn* —1A **20**
Sudbourne. *Suff* —1D **35**

Sudbrook. *Linc* —1A **4**
Sudbury. *Suff* —2B **32**
Suffield. *Norf* —2B **10**
Summerfield. *Norf* —2A **8**
Sundon Park. *Lutn* —1B **36**
Surfleet. *Linc* —3D **5**
Surfleet Seas End. *Linc*
—3D **5**
Surlingham. *Norf* —2C **19**
Surrex. *Essx* —1B **40**
Sustead. *Norf* —2A **10**
Suton. *Norf* —3D **17**
Sutterton. *Linc* —2D **5**
Sutterton Dowdyke. *Linc*
—2D **5**
Sutton. *Beds* —2D **29**
Sutton. *Cambs* —2B **22**
Sutton. *Norf* —3C **11**
Sutton. *Pet* —3B **12**
Sutton. *Suff* —2C **35**
Sutton Bridge. *Linc* —3B **6**
Sutton Corner. *Linc* —3B **6**
Sutton Crosses. *Linc* —3B **6**
Sutton Gault. *Cambs*
—2B **22**
Sutton St Edmund. *Linc*
—1A **14**
Sutton St Edmund's
Common. *Linc* —2A **14**
Sutton St James. *Linc*
—1A **14**
Swaffham. *Norf* —2B **16**
Swaffham Bulbeck. *Cambs*
—3C **23**
Swaffham Prior. *Cambs*
—3C **23**
Swafield. *Norf* —2B **10**
Swainsthorpe. *Norf* —2B **18**
Swannington. *Norf* —1A **18**
Swan Street. *Essx* —1B **40**
Swanton Abbot. *Norf*
—3B **10**
Swanton Morley. *Norf*
—1D **17**
Swanton Novers. *Norf*
—2D **9**
Swarby. *Linc* —1B **4**
Swardeston. *Norf* —2B **18**
Swaton. *Linc* —2C **5**
Swavesey. *Cambs* —3A **22**
Swayfield. *Linc* —3A **4**
Swefling. *Suff* —3C **27**
Swilland. *Suff* —1A **34**
Swineshead. *Beds* —3B **20**
Swineshead. *Linc* —1D **5**
Swineshead Bridge. *Linc*
—1D **5**
Swingbrow. *Cambs* —1A **22**
Swingleton Green. *Suff*
—2C **33**
Swinstead. *Linc* —3B **4**
Syderstone. *Norf* —2B **8**
Syleham. *Suff* —2B **26**
Syston. *Linc* —1A **4**

Tacolneston. *Norf* —3A **18**
Tadlow. *Cambs* —2D **29**
Takeley. *Essx* —1C **39**
Takeley Street. *Essx* —1C **39**
Tallington. *Linc* —2B **12**
Tamworth Green. *Linc*
—1A **6**
Tannington. *Suff* —3B **26**
Tan Office Green. *Suff*
—1A **32**
Tansor. *Nptn* —3B **12**

Tasburgh. *Norf* —3B **18**
Tatterford. *Norf* —3B **8**
Tattersett. *Norf* —2B **8**
Tattingstone. *Suff* —3A **34**
Tattingstone White Horse.
  Suff —3A **34**
Taverham. *Norf* —1A **18**
Taverners Green. *Essx*
  —2C **39**
Tebworth. *Beds* —1A **36**
Teigh. *Rut* —1A **12**
Tempsford. *Beds* —1C **29**
Tendring. *Essx* —1A **42**
Tendring Green. *Essx*
  —1A **42**
Ten Mile Bank. *Norf* —3D **15**
Terling. *Essx* —2A **40**
Terrick. *Buck* —3A **36**
Terrington St Clement. *Norf*
  —3C **7**
Terrington St John. *Norf*
  —1C **15**
Teversham. *Cambs* —1B **30**
Tewin. *Herts* —2D **37**
Tharston. *Norf* —3A **18**
Thaxted. *Essx* —3D **31**
Theberton. *Suff* —3D **27**
Thelnetham. *Suff* —2D **25**
Thelveton. *Norf* —1A **26**
Themelthorpe. *Norf* —3D **9**
Therfield. *Herts* —3A **30**
Thetford. *Linc* —1C **13**
Thetford. *Norf* —1B **24**
Theydon Bois. *Essx* —3B **38**
Thistleton. *Rut* —1A **12**
Thistley Green. *Suff* —2D **23**
Tholomas Drove. *Cambs*
  —2B **14**
Thompson. *Norf* —3C **17**
Thorington. *Suff* —2D **27**
Thorington Street. *Suff*
  —3D **33**
Thorley. *Herts* —2B **38**
Thorley Street. *Herts*
  —2B **38**
Thornage. *Norf* —2D **9**
Thorncote Green. *Beds*
  —2C **29**
Thorndon. *Suff* —3A **26**
Thorney. *Pet* —2D **13**
Thorney Toll. *Cambs* —2A **14**
Thornham. *Norf* —1A **8**
Thornham Magna. *Suff*
  —2A **26**
Thornham Parva. *Suff*
  —2A **26**
Thornhaugh. *Pet* —2B **12**
Thorns. *Suff* —1A **32**
Thornwood Common. *Essx*
  —3B **38**
Thorpe. *Norf* —3D **19**
Thorpe Abbotts. *Norf*
  —2A **26**
Thorpe by Water. *Rut*
  —3A **12**
Thorpe Common. *Suff*
  —3B **34**
Thorpe End. *Norf* —1B **18**
Thorpe Green. *Essx* —1A **42**
Thorpe Green. *Suff* —1C **33**
Thorpe Hamlet. *Norf* —2B **18**
Thorpe Latimer. *Linc* —1C **5**
Thorpe-le-Soken. *Essx*
  —1A **42**
Thorpe Market. *Norf* —2B **10**
Thorpe Marriott. *Norf*
  —1A **18**

Thorpe Morieux. *Suff*
  —1C **33**
Thorpeness. *Suff* —2B **27**
Thorpe Waterville. *Nptn*
  —1B **20**
Thorpland. *Norf* —2D **15**
Thorrington. *Essx* —1D **41**
Thrandeston. *Suff* —2A **26**
Thrapston. *Nptn* —2A **20**
Three Holes. *Norf* —2C **15**
Threekingham. *Linc* —2B **4**
Thrigby. *Norf* —1D **19**
Thriplow. *Cambs* —2B **30**
Throckenholt. *Linc* —2A **14**
Throcking. *Herts* —3A **30**
Thurgarton. *Norf* —2A **10**
Thurlby. *Linc* —1C **13**
Thurleigh. *Beds* —1B **28**
Thurlton. *Norf* —3D **19**
Thurne. *Norf* —1D **19**
Thurning. *Norf* —3D **9**
Thurning. *Nptn* —1B **20**
Thursford. *Norf* —2C **9**
Thursford Green. *Norf*
  —2C **9**
Thurston. *Suff* —3C **25**
Thurston End. *Suff* —1A **32**
Thurton. *Norf* —2C **19**
Thuxton. *Norf* —2D **17**
Thwaite. *Suff* —3A **26**
Thwaite St Mary. *Norf*
  —3C **19**
Tibenham. *Norf* —1A **26**
Tickencote. *Rut* —2A **12**
Tilbrook. *Cambs* —3B **20**
Tillingham. *Essx* —3C **41**
Tilney All Saints. *Norf*
  —1C **15**
Tilney Fen Side. *Norf*
  —1C **15**
Tilney High End. *Norf*
  —1C **15**
Tilney St Lawrence. *Norf*
  —1C **15**
Tilsworth. *Beds* —1A **36**
Timworth Green. *Suff*
  —3B **24**
Tingrith. *Beds* —3B **28**
Tinwell. *Rut* —2B **12**
Tips End. *Cambs* —3C **15**
Tiptree. *Essx* —2B **40**
Tiptree Heath. *Essx* —2B **40**
Titchmarsh. *Nptn* —2B **20**
Titchwell. *Norf* —1A **8**
Tittleshall. *Norf* —3B **8**
Tivetshall St Margaret. *Norf*
  —1A **26**
Tivetshall St Mary. *Norf*
  —1A **26**
Tixover. *Rut* —2A **12**
Toddington. *Beds* —1B **36**
Toft. *Cambs* —1A **30**
Toft. *Linc* —1B **12**
Toft Monks. *Norf* —3D **19**
Toftrees. *Norf* —3B **8**
Toftwood. *Norf* —1C **17**
Tollesbury. *Essx* —2C **41**
Tolleshunt D'Arcy. *Essx*
  —2C **41**
Tolleshunt Knights. *Essx*
  —2C **41**
Tolleshunt Major. *Essx*
  —2C **41**
Tonwell. *Herts* —2A **38**
Toot Hill. *Essx* —3C **39**
Topcroft. *Norf* —3B **18**
Topcroft Street. *Norf* —3B **18**

Toppesfield. *Essx* —3A **32**
Toprow. *Norf* —3A **18**
Toseland. *Cambs* —3D **21**
Tostock. *Suff* —3C **25**
Tottenhill. *Norf* —1D **15**
Tottenhill Row. *Norf* —1D **15**
Totternhoe. *Beds* —1A **36**
Tower End. *Norf* —1D **15**
Town End. *Cambs* —3B **14**
Towngate. *Linc* —1C **13**
Townsend. *Herts* —3C **37**
Town Street. *Suff* —1A **24**
Trimingham. *Norf* —2B **10**
Trimley Lower Street. *Suff*
  —3B **34**
Trimley St Mary. *Suff*
  —3B **34**
Tring. *Herts* —2A **36**
Troston. *Suff* —2B **24**
Trowley Bottom. *Herts*
  —2B **36**
Trowse Newton. *Norf*
  —2B **18**
Trumpington. *Cambs*
  —1B **30**
Trunch. *Norf* —2B **10**
Tuddenham. *Suff* —2A **34**
  (nr. Ipswich)
Tuddenham. *Suff* —2A **24**
  (nr. Mildenhall)
Tumbler's Green. *Essx*
  —1B **40**
Tungate. *Norf* —3B **10**
Tunstall. *Norf* —2D **19**
Tunstall. *Suff* —1C **35**
Tunstead. *Norf* —3B **10**
Turnford. *Herts* —3A **38**
Turvey. *Beds* —1A **28**
Tuttington. *Norf* —3B **10**
Twenty. *Linc* —3C **5**
Twinstead. *Essx* —3B **32**
Twinstead Green. *Essx*
  —3B **32**
Twyford. *Norf* —3D **9**
Twywell. *Nptn* —2A **20**
Tyby. *Norf* —3D **9**
Tydd Gote. *Linc* —1B **14**
Tydd St Giles. *Cambs*
  —1B **14**
Tydd St Mary. *Linc* —1B **14**
Tye Green. *Essx* —1C **39**
  (nr. Bishop's Stortford)
Tye Green. *Essx* —1A **40**
  (nr. Braintree)
Tye Green. *Essx* —3C **31**
  (nr. Saffron Walden)
Tyler's Green. *Essx* —3C **39**
Tyringham. *Mil* —2A **28**

Ubbeston Green. *Suff*
  —2C **27**
Uffington. *Linc* —2B **12**
Ufford. *Pet* —2B **12**
Ufford. *Suff* —1B **34**
Uggeshall. *Suff* —2D **27**
Ugley. *Essx* —1C **39**
Ugley Green. *Essx* —1C **39**
Ulting. *Essx* —3B **40**
Undley. *Suff* —1D **23**
Upend. *Cambs* —1A **32**
Upgate. *Norf* —1A **18**
Upgate Street. *Norf* —3D **17**
Upper Benefield. *Nptn*
  —1A **20**
Upper Caldecote. *Beds*
  —2C **29**

Upper Dean. *Beds* —3B **20**
Upper Dovercourt. *Essx*
  —3B **34**
Upper Dunsley. *Herts*
  —2A **36**
Upper Gravenhurst. *Beds*
  —3C **29**
Upper Green. *Essx* —3B **30**
Upper Hambleton. *Rut*
  —2A **12**
Upper Hellesdon. *Norf*
  —1B **18**
Upper Layham. *Suff* —2D **33**
Upper North Dean. *Buck*
  —3A **36**
Upper Shelton. *Beds* —2A **28**
Upper Sheringham. *Norf*
  —1A **10**
Upper StAploe. *Beds* —1C **29**
Upper Stoke. *Norf* —2B **18**
Upper Stondon. *Beds*
  —3C **29**
Upper Street. *Norf* —1C **19**
  (nr. Horning)
Upper Street. *Norf* —1C **19**
  (nr. Hoveton)
Upper Street. *Suff* —3A **34**
Upper Sundon. *Beds*
  —1B **36**
Uppingham. *Rut* —3A **12**
Upshire. *Essx* —3B **38**
Upthorpe. *Suff* —2C **25**
Upton. *Cambs* —2C **21**
Upton. *Norf* —1C **19**
Upton. *Pet* —2C **13**
Upton End. *Beds* —3C **29**
Upware. *Cambs* —2C **23**
Upwell. *Cambs* —2B **14**
Upwick Green. *Herts* —1B **38**
Upwood. *Cambs* —1D **21**

Wacton. *Norf* —3A **18**
Wadenhoe. *Nptn* —1B **20**
Wadesmill. *Herts* —2A **38**
Wakerley. *Nptn* —3A **12**
Wakes Colne. *Essx* —1B **40**
Walberswick. *Suff* —2D **27**
Walcot. *Linc* —2B **4**
Walcot Green. *Norf* —1A **26**
Walcott. *Norf* —2C **11**
Waldringfield. *Suff* —2B **34**
Walkern. *Herts* —1D **37**
Wallington. *Herts* —3D **29**
Walpole. *Suff* —2C **27**
Walpole Cross Keys. *Norf*
  —1C **15**
Walpole Gate. *Norf* —1C **15**
Walpole Highway. *Norf*
  —1C **15**
Walpolelane. *Suff* —2C **27**
Walpole Marsh. *Norf*
  —1B **14**
Walpole St Andrew. *Norf*
  —1C **15**
Walpole St Peter. *Norf*
  —1C **15**
Walsham le Willows. *Suff*
  —2D **25**
Walsoken. *Cambs* —1B **14**
Walsworth. *Herts* —3C **29**
Waltham Abbey. *Essx*
  —3A **38**
Waltham Cross. *Herts*
  —3A **38**
Waltham's Cross. *Essx*
  —3D **31**

Walton. *Mil* —3A **28**
Walton. *Pet* —2C **13**
Walton. *Suff* —3B **34**
Walton Highway. *Norf*
  —1B **14**
Walton-on-the-Naze. *Essx*
  —1B **42**
Wangford. *Suff* —1A **24**
  (nr. Lakenheath)
Wangford. *Suff* —2D **27**
  (nr. Southwold)
Wansford. *Cambs* —3B **12**
Warboys. *Cambs* —1A **22**
Ward Green. *Suff* —3D **25**
Wardhedges. *Beds* —3B **28**
Wardy Hill. *Cambs* —1B **22**
Ware. *Herts* —2A **38**
Wareside. *Herts* —2A **38**
Waresley. *Cambs* —1D **29**
Wargate. *Linc* —2D **5**
Warham. *Norf* —1C **9**
Warkton. *Nptn* —2A **20**
Warmington. *Nptn* —3B **12**
Warners End. *Herts* —3B **36**
Warrington. *Mil* —1A **28**
Washbrook. *Suff* —2A **34**
Waterbeach. *Cambs* —3B **22**
Waterden. *Norf* —2B **8**
Water End. *Beds* —3B **28**
Water End. *Herts* —3D **37**
  (nr. Hatfield)
Water End. *Herts* —2B **36**
  (nr. Hemel Hempstead)
Waterford. *Herts* —2A **38**
Waterloo. *Norf* —1B **18**
Water Newton. *Cambs*
  —3C **13**
Waterside. *Buck* —3A **36**
Waterside. *Cambs* —2D **23**
Watford. *Herts* —3B **36**
Watlington. *Norf* —1D **15**
Wattisfield. *Suff* —2D **25**
Wattisham. *Suff* —1D **33**
Watton. *Norf* —2C **17**
Watton at Stone. *Herts*
  —2D **37**
Wavendon. *Mil* —3A **28**
Waxham. *Norf* —3D **11**
Way Head. *Cambs* —1B **22**
Weasenham All Saints. *Norf*
  —3B **8**
Weasenham St Peter. *Norf*
  —3B **8**
Weekley. *Nptn* —1A **20**
Weeley. *Essx* —1A **42**
Weeley Heath. *Essx* —1A **42**
Weeting. *Norf* —1A **24**
Welborne. *Norf* —1D **17**
Welby. *Linc* —2A **4**
Welches Dam. *Cambs*
  —1B **22**
Weldon. *Nptn* —1A **20**
Welham Green. *Herts*
  —3D **37**
Wellingborough. *Nptn*
  —3A **20**
Wellingham. *Norf* —3B **8**
Wellpond Green. *Herts*
  —1B **38**
Wells-next-the-Sea. *Norf*
  —1C **9**
Welney. *Norf* —3C **15**
Welwyn. *Herts* —2D **37**
Welwyn Garden City. *Herts*
  —2D **37**
Wendens Ambo. *Essx*
  —3C **31**

Wending. *Norf* —1C **17**
Wendover. *Buck* —3A **36**
Wendy. *Cambs* —2A **30**
Wenhaston. *Suff* —2D **27**
Wennington. *Cambs* —2D **21**
Wentworth. *Cambs* —2B **22**
Wereham. *Norf* —2D **15**
Werrington. *Pet* —2C **13**
West Acre. *Norf* —1A **16**
West Barsham. *Norf* —2C **9**
West Beckham. *Norf* —1A **10**
West Bergholt. *Essx* —1C **41**
West Bilney. *Norf* —1A **16**
Westborough. *Linc* —1A **4**
West Bradenham. *Norf*
—2C **17**
West Briggs. *Norf* —1D **15**
Westby. *Linc* —3A **4**
West Caister. *Norf* —1D **19**
West Deeping. *Linc* —2C **13**
West Dereham. *Norf* —2D **15**
West End. *Beds* —1A **28**
West End. *Cambs* —3B **14**
West End. *Herts* —3D **37**
West End. *Linc* —1A **6**
West End. *Norf* —1D **19**
Westerfield. *Suff* —2A **34**
Westfield. *Norf* —2C **17**
Westgate. *Norf* —1C **9**
Westhall. *Suff* —1D **27**
West Hanningfield. *Essx*
—3A **40**
West Head. *Norf* —2C **15**
Westhorpe. *Linc* —2D **5**
Westhorpe. *Suff* —3D **25**
West Leith. *Herts* —2A **36**
Westleton. *Suff* —3D **27**
West Lexham. *Norf* —1B **16**
Westley. *Suff* —3B **24**
Westley Waterless. *Cambs*
—1D **31**
West Lynn. *Norf* —1D **15**
West Mersea. *Essx* —2D **41**
Westmill. *Herts* —1A **38**
(nr. Buntingford)
Westmill. *Herts* —3C **29**
(nr. Hitchin)
West Newton. *Norf* —3D **7**
Weston. *Herts* —3D **29**
Weston. *Linc* —3D **5**
Weston. *Suff* —1D **27**
Weston Colville. *Cambs*
—1D **31**
Weston Ditch. *Suff* —2D **23**
Weston Green. *Cambs*
—1D **31**
Weston Green. *Norf* —1A **18**
Weston Hills. *Linc* —1D **13**
Westoning. *Beds* —3B **28**
Weston Longville. *Norf*
—1A **18**
Weston Turville. *Buck*
—2A **36**
Weston Underwood. *Mil*
—1A **28**

West Perry. *Cambs* —3C **21**
West Poringland. *Norf*
—2B **18**
West Raynham. *Norf* —3B **8**
West Row. *Suff* —2D **23**
West Rudham. *Norf* —3B **8**
West Runton. *Norf* —1A **10**
Westry. *Cambs* —3A **14**
West Somerton. *Norf*
—1D **19**
West Stow. *Suff* —2B **24**
West Tofts. *Norf* —3B **16**
West Walton. *Norf* —1B **14**
Westwick. *Cambs* —3B **22**
Westwick. *Norf* —3B **10**
West Wickham. *Cambs*
—2D **31**
West Willoughby. *Linc*
—1A **4**
West Winch. *Norf* —1D **15**
Westwood. *Pet* —3C **13**
West Wratting. *Cambs*
—1D **31**
Wetherden. *Suff* —3D **25**
Wetheringsett. *Suff* —3A **26**
Wethersfield. *Essx* —3A **32**
Wetherup Street. *Suff*
—3A **26**
Weybourne. *Norf* —1A **10**
Weybread. *Suff* —1B **26**
Whaddon. *Cambs* —2A **30**
Whaplode. *Linc* —3A **6**
Whaplode Drove. *Linc*
—1A **14**
Whaplode St Catherine. *Linc*
—3A **6**
Wharley End. *Beds* —2A **28**
Whatfield. *Suff* —2D **33**
Wheatacre. *Norf* —3D **19**
Wheathampstead. *Herts*
—2C **37**
Whelpley Hill. *Buck* —3A **36**
Whepstead. *Suff* —1B **32**
Wherstead. *Suff* —2A **34**
Whimpwell Green. *Norf*
—3C **11**
Whinburgh. *Norf* —2D **17**
Whipsnade. *Beds* —2B **36**
Whissonsett. *Norf* —3C **9**
Whiston. *Nptn* —3A **20**
Whiteash Green. *Essx*
—3A **32**
White Colne. *Essx* —1B **40**
White Horse Common. *Norf*
—3C **11**
White Notley. *Essx* —2A **40**
White Roding. *Essx* —2C **39**
Whitestreet Green. *Suff*
—3C **33**
Whitington. *Norf* —3A **16**
Whittlesey. *Cambs* —3D **13**
Whittlesford. *Cambs* —2B **30**
Whitwell. *Herts* —1C **37**
Whitwell. *Rut* —2A **12**
Wicken. *Cambs* —2C **23**

Wicken Bonhunt. *Essx*
—3B **30**
Wicker Street Green. *Suff*
—2C **33**
Wickham Bishops. *Essx*
—2B **40**
Wickhambrook. *Suff* —1A **32**
Wickham Green. *Suff*
—3D **25**
Wickham Market. *Suff*
—1B **34**
Wickhampton. *Norf* —2D **19**
Wickham St Paul. *Essx*
—3B **32**
Wickham Skeith. *Suff*
—3D **25**
Wickham Street. *Suff*
—3D **25**
Wicklewood. *Norf* —2D **17**
Wickmere. *Norf* —2A **10**
Widdington. *Essx* —3C **31**
Widford. *Essx* —3D **39**
Widford. *Herts* —2B **38**
Widmer End. *Buck* —3A **36**
Wiggenhall St Germans. *Norf*
—1C **15**
Wiggenhall St Mary
Magdalen. *Norf* —1C **15**
Wiggenhall St Mary the
Virgin. *Norf* —1C **15**
Wiggenhall St Peter. *Norf*
—1D **15**
Wiggens Green. *Essx*
—2D **31**
Wigginton. *Herts* —2A **36**
Wighton. *Norf* —1C **9**
Wigsthorpe. *Nptn* —1B **20**
Wigtoft. *Linc* —2D **5**
Wilburton. *Cambs* —2B **22**
Wilby. *Norf* —3D **17**
Wilby. *Nptn* —3A **20**
Wilby. *Suff* —2B **26**
Wilden. *Beds* —1B **28**
Wilde Street. *Suff* —2A **24**
Willen. *Mil* —2A **28**
Willian. *Herts* —3D **29**
Willingale. *Essx* —3C **39**
Willingham. *Cambs* —2B **22**
Willingham Green. *Cambs*
—1D **31**
Willington. *Beds* —2C **29**
Willisham Tye. *Suff* —1D **33**
Willows Green. *Essx* —2A **40**
Wilney Green. *Norf* —1D **25**
Wilsford. *Linc* —1B **4**
Wilstead. *Beds* —2B **28**
Wilsthorpe. *Linc* —1B **12**
Wilstone. *Herts* —2A **36**
Wimbish. *Essx* —3C **31**
Wimbish Green. *Essx*
—3D **31**
Wimblington. *Cambs*
—3B **14**
Wimbotsham. *Norf* —2D **15**
Windsor Green. *Suff* —1B **32**

Winfarthing. *Norf* —1A **26**
Wing. *Buck* —1A **36**
Wing. *Rut* —2A **12**
Wingfield. *Beds* —1B **36**
Wingfield. *Suff* —2B **26**
Wingrave. *Buck* —2A **36**
Winston. *Suff* —3A **26**
Winterton-on-Sea. *Norf*
—1D **19**
Winwick. *Cambs* —1C **21**
Wisbech. *Cambs* —1B **14**
Wisbech St Mary. *Cambs*
—2B **14**
Wissett. *Suff* —2C **27**
Wistow. *Cambs* —1D **21**
Witcham. *Cambs* —1B **22**
Witchford. *Cambs* —2C **23**
Witham. *Essx* —2B **40**
Witham on the Hill. *Linc*
—1B **12**
Withergate. *Norf* —3B **10**
Withermarsh Green. *Suff*
—3D **33**
Withersdale Street. *Suff*
—1B **26**
Withersfield. *Suff* —2D **31**
Witnesham. *Suff* —1A **34**
Wittering. *Pet* —2B **12**
Witton. *Norf* —2C **19**
Witton Bridge. *Norf* —2C **11**
Wivenhoe. *Essx* —1D **41**
Wiveton. *Norf* —1D **9**
Wix. *Essx* —1A **42**
Wixoe. *Suff* —2A **32**
Woburn. *Beds* —3A **28**
Woburn Sands. *Mil* —3A **28**
Wolferton. *Norf* —3D **7**
Wollaston. *Nptn* —3A **20**
Wolterton. *Norf* —2A **10**
Woodbastwick. *Norf* —1C **19**
Woodbridge. *Suff* —2B **34**
Wood Dalling. *Norf* —3D **9**
Woodditton. *Cambs* —1D **31**
Wood End. *Herts* —1A **38**
Woodend Green. *Essx*
—1C **39**
Woodford. *Nptn* —2A **20**
Woodgate. *Norf* —1D **17**
Woodham Ferrers. *Essx*
—3A **40**
Woodham Mortimer. *Essx*
—3B **40**
Woodham Walter. *Essx*
—3B **40**
Woodhurst. *Cambs* —2A **22**
Woodnewton. *Nptn* —3B **12**
Woodnook. *Linc* —2A **4**
Wood Norton. *Norf* —3D **9**
Woodrising. *Norf* —2C **17**
Woodside. *Herts* —3D **37**
Woodston. *Pet* —3C **13**
Woodton. *Norf* —3B **18**
Woodwalton. *Cambs*
—1D **21**
Woolley. *Cambs* —2C **21**

Woolmer Green. *Herts*
—2D **37**
Woolpit. *Suff* —3C **25**
Woolsthorpe. *Linc* —3A **4**
(nr. Colsterworth)
Woolsthorpe. *Linc* —2A **4**
(nr. Grantham)
Woolverstone. *Suff* —3A **34**
Wootton. *Beds* —2B **28**
Workhouse Green. *Suff*
—3C **33**
Worlingham. *Suff* —3D **19**
Worlington. *Suff* —2D **23**
Worlingworth. *Suff* —3B **26**
Wormegay. *Norf* —1D **15**
Wormingford. *Essx* —3C **33**
Wormley. *Herts* —3A **38**
Worstead. *Norf* —3C **11**
Wortham. *Suff* —2D **25**
Worthing. *Norf* —1C **17**
Wortwell. *Norf* —1B **26**
Wothorpe. *Nptn* —2B **12**
Wrabness. *Essx* —3A **34**
Wramplingham. *Norf*
—2A **18**
Wrangle. *Linc* —1B **6**
Wrangle Lowgate. *Linc*
—1B **6**
Wreningham. *Norf* —3A **18**
Wrentham. *Suff* —1D **27**
Wrestlingworth. *Beds*
—2D **29**
Wretham. *Norf* —3C **17**
Wretton. *Norf* —2D **15**
Wright's Green. *Essx*
—2C **39**
Writtle. *Essx* —3D **39**
Wroxham. *Norf* —1C **19**
Wyatt's Green. *Essx* —3C **39**
Wyberton. *Linc* —1A **6**
Wyboston. *Beds* —1C **29**
Wyddial. *Herts* —3A **30**
Wykeham. *Linc* —3D **5**
Wymington. *Beds* —3A **20**
Wymondham. *Leics* —1A **12**
Wymondham. *Norf* —2A **18**
Wyton. *Cambs* —2D **21**
Wyverstone. *Suff* —3D **25**
Wyverstone Street. *Suff*
—3D **25**
Wyville. *Linc* —3A **4**

Yardley Hastings. *Nptn*
—1A **28**
Yarwell. *Nptn* —3B **12**
Yaxham. *Norf* —1D **17**
Yaxley. *Cambs* —3C **13**
Yaxley. *Suff* —2A **26**
Yelden. *Beds* —3B **20**
Yelling. *Cambs* —3D **21**
Yelverton. *Norf* —2B **18**
Young's End. *Essx* —2A **40**
Yoxford. *Suff* —3C **27**

Selected Places of Interest and other features

❏ Opening times for Places of Interest vary greatly; while some open all year, others open only for the summer season, some only open certain days or even part days. We recommend, to avoid disappointment, you check with the nearest Tourist Information Centre (see pages 63/64) before starting your journey.

❏ This is an index to selected features shown on the map pages, it is not a comprehensive guide.

❏ To keep the maps as clear as possible, descriptive words like 'Castle', 'Museum' etc. are omitted, a key to the various map symbols used can be found on page 1 in the reference. Features within very congested areas and town centres are indicated as space allows, wherever possible, at least with the appropriate symbol; in some instances the text may fall into an adjacent map square.

❏ Every possible care has been taken to ensure that the information given in this publication is accurate and whilst the publishers would be grateful to learn of any errors, they regret they cannot accept any responsibility for loss thereby caused.

Abbey/Friary/Priory

Beeston Priory, Beeston Regis
—1A **10**

Binham Priory —1C **9**
Burnham Norton Friary,
Burnham Market —1B **8**
Bury St Edmunds Abbey —3B **24**
Bushmead Priory —3C **21**
Castle Acre Priory —1B **16**
Clare Priory —2A **32**
Creake Abbey, North Creake —2B **8**
Denny Abbey, Denny End —3B **22**
Dunwich Greyfriars —2D **27**
Greyfriars' Cloisters, Great Yarmouth
—2D **19**
Greyfriars Tower, King's Lynn —1D **15**
Leiston Abbey —3D **27**
Ramsey Abbey —1D **21**
Royston Priory & St John the
Baptist Church —2A **30**
St Benet's Abbey, Johnson's Street
—1C **19**
St Botolph's Priory, Colchester
—1D **41**
St Faith's Priory, Horsham St Faith
—1B **18**
St Leonard's Priory, Stamford —2B **12**
St Olaves Priory —3D **19**
St Osyth Priory —2A **42**
Thetford Priory —1B **24**
Walsingham Abbey & Priory,
Little Walsingham —2C **9**
Ware Priory —2A **38**
Weybourne Priory —1A **10**

Wymondham Abbey & Church
—2A **18**

Aquarium

Great Yarmouth Sea Life Centre
—2D **19**
Hunstanton Sea Life Centre —1D **7**
Mickfield Fish & Water Garden
—3A **26**
Waveney Fish Farm, Diss —2A **26**

Arboretum

See also Garden

Barnsdale Arboretum, Whitwell
—2A **12**
Blakenham Woodland Garden,
Little Blakenham —2A **34**
Lynford Arboretum, Mundford —3B **16**
Whipsnade Tree Cathedral —2B **36**

Bird Garden

See also Farm Park, Wildlife Park, Zoo

Peakirk Wildfowl Gardens —2C **13**
Stagsden Bird Gardens —2A **28**
Pensthorpe Waterfowl Park,
Falkenham —3C **9**
Woodside Wildfowl Park & Farm,
Aley Green —2B **36**

Botanical Garden

Cambridge University Botanic Garden
—1B **30**

Spalding Tropical Forest, Pinchbeck
—3D **5**

Broads Authority Information Centres

*See also Tourist Information
Centres NOTE: Telephone
Numbers are given in Italics*

Beccles —3D **19** *01502 713196*
Hoveton —1C **19** *01603 782281*
Ranworth —1C **19** *01603 270453*
Toad Hole Cottage, How Hill —1C **19**
01692 678763

Butterfly Farm

Barrow Tropical Butterfly Garden
—3A **24**
Hopton Butterfly & Bird World,
Hopton on Sea —3D **19**
Long Sutton Butterfly & Falconry Park,
Little London —3B **6**
Rutland Water Butterfly &
Aquatic Centre, Empingham —2A **12**

Castle

See also Castle & Garden

Anstey Castle —3B **30**
Baconsthorpe Castle —2A **10**
Bedford Castle —2B **28**
Benington Castle —1D **37**
Berkhamsted Castle —3A **36**
Bourne Castle —1B **12**
Bungay Castle —1C **27**
Burwell Castle —3C **23**
Caister Castle, West Caister —1D **19**

Cambridge Castle (Castle Mound)
—1B **30**

Castle Acre Castle —1B **16**
Castle Rising Castle —3D **7**
Clare Castle —2A **32**
Colchester Castle —1C **41**
Eaton Socon Castle —1C **29**
Ely Castle —2C **23**
Eye Castle —2A **26**
Fotheringhay Castle —3B **12**
Framlingham Castle —3B **26**
Haughley Castle —3D **25**
Hedingham Castle, Castle Hedingham
—3A **32**

Hertford Castle —2A **38**
Horsford Castle —1B **18**
Huntingdon Castle —2D **21**
Lavendon Castle —1A **28**
Lidgate Castle —1A **32**
New Buckenham Castle —3D **17**
Norwich Castle —2B **18**
Oakham Castle —2A **12**
Ongar Castle, Chipping Ongar
—3C **39**

Orford Castle —2D **35**
Pleshey Castle —2D **39**
Saffron Walden Castle —3C **31**
Someries Castle, Chiltern Green
—2C **37**

Stansted Mountfitchet Castle —1C **39**
Swineshead Castle, Baythorpe —1D **5**
Thetford Castle —1B **24**
Totternhoe Castle —1A **36**
Weeting Castle —1A **24**
Weston Turville Castle —2A **36**
Woodwalton Castle, Church End
—1D **21**

Castle & Garden
See also Castle

Rockingham Castle —3A **12**

Cathedral
Bury St Edmunds Cathedral —3B **24**
Chelmsford Cathedral —3A **40**
Ely Cathedral —1C **23**
North Elmham Saxon Cathedral &
Bishop's Castle —3C **9**
Norwich Cathedral —2B **18**
Norwich RC Cathedral —2B **18**
Peterborough Cathedral —3C **13**
St Albans Cathedral & Abbey Church
—3C **37**

Cave
Royston Cave —2A **30**
Scott's Grotto, Ware —2A **38**

Country Park
Barnwell Country Park, Oundle
—1B **20**
Brandon Country Park —1A **24**
Brigstock Country Park —1A **20**
Clare Castle Country Park —2A **32**
Cudmore Grove Country Park,
East Mersea —2D **41**
Danbury Country Park —3A **40**
Dunstable Downs Country Park
—2B **36**
Easton Farm Park —1B **34**
Emberton Country Park —1A **28**
Ferry Meadows Country Park,
Peterborough —3C **13**
Fritton Lake Country Park —2D **19**
Great Cornard Country Park —3B **32**
Harrold-Odell Country Park —1A **28**
Hatfield Forest Country Park,
Takeley Street —2C **39**
High Woods Country Park, Mile End
—1D **41**
Hinchingbrooke Country Park,
Huntingdon —2D **21**
Holland Haven Country Park,
Holland-on-Sea —2B **42**
Holt Woodlands Country Park —2D **9**
Irchester Country Park —3A **20**
Knebworth Country Park,
Old Knebworth —1D **37**
Knettishall Heath Country Park,
Rushford —1C **25**
Lee Valley Park, Waltham Cross
—3A **38**
Lonely Farm Leisure Park,
Saxmundham —3C **27**
Marsh Farm Country Park, South
Woodham Ferrers —3B **40**
Northaw Great Wood Country Park
—3D **37**
Priory Country Park, Bedford —2B **28**
Rutland Water Country Park —2A **12**
Sandringham Country Park —3D **7**
Stewartby Lake Country Park —2B **28**
Stockgrove Country Park,
Great Brickhill —1A **36**
Sundon Hills Country Park,
Upper Sundon —1B **36**
Trent Park Country Park, Cockfosters
—3D **37**

Wandlebury Country Park, Cambridge
—1B **30**
West Stow Country Park —2A **24**

Farm Park/Working Farm
See also Wildlife Park

Bowmans Open Farm, London Colney
—3C **37**
Bury Farm Centre, Epping —3B **38**
Cranes Watering Farm, Harleston
—1B **26**
Dedham Rare Breeds Farm —3D **33**
Gray's Honey Farm, Chatteris —1A **22**
Hayes Hill Farm, Holyfield —3A **38**
Marsh Farm, South Woodham Ferrers
—3B **40**
Oak Farm Rare Breeds Park,
Aylesbury —2A **36**
Park Farm, Snettisham —2D **7**
Rutland Farm Park, Oakham —2A **12**
Stags Holt Farm Park, Chainbridge
—2B **14**
Standalone Farm Centre, Letchworth
—3D **29**
Teddy's Farm, Beckingham —1A **4**
Union Farm, Gressenhall —1C **17**
Water Hall Farm & Craft Centre,
Whitwell —1C **37**

Fortress
Felixstowe 'Q' Tower —3B **34**
Harwich Redoubt —3B **34**
Landguard Fort, Felixstowe —3B **34**
Martello Tower No. 1, Point Clear
—2D **41**

Garden
*See also Historic Building &
Garden*

Akenfield Garden, Charsfield —1B **34**
Alby Gardens, Erpingham —2B **10**
Barnsdale Drought Garden, Whitwell
—2A **12**
BBC Essex Garden, Abridge —3B **38**
Benington Lordship Gardens —1D **37**
Beth Chatto Gardens, Elmstead
Market —1D **41**
Blake Hall Gardens, Bobbingworth
—3C **39**
Bressingham Dell Garden —1D **25**
Bridge End Gardens, Saffron Walden
—3C **31**